Crime and Conflict in Northern Ireland, 1920–2022

D1614491

Studies in Irish Crime History

Crime and Conflict in Northern Ireland, 1920–2022

Aogán Mulcahy

CORK UNIVERSITY PRESS

First published in 2023 by
Cork University Press
Boole Library
University College Cork
Cork T12 ND89
Ireland

Library of Congress Control Number: 2023942972

Distribution in the USA Longleaf Services, Chapel Hill, NC, USA.

British Library Cataloguing in Publication Data
A CIP catalogue record for this book is available the British Library.

ISBN 9781782055730

Printed by Hussar Books in Poland

Design and typesetting by Alison Burns at Studio 10 Design, Cork

Cover image: A man is tarred and feathered for theft in Northern Ireland,
1971. Trinity Mirror/Mirrorpix

www.corkuniversitypress.com

MIX
Paper from
responsible sources
FSC
www.fsc.org   FSC® C167221

Contents

Studies in Irish Crime History

SERIES EDITORS: Richard Mc Mahon and Ciara Molloy

This book series explores how crime history can offer new ways of understanding Irish society. It maps and critically engages with the actions and beliefs of those who often held a marginal position in Irish society, their relationship to the broader population and, crucially, their interactions with those in positions of authority. The history of the murderer, the prostitute, the thief, the bank robber, the vagrant, the white-collar criminal, among others, and their relationship to the police officer, the lawyer, the jury, the judge and the hangman will be explored to arrive at a deeper sense of the conflicts and contradictions that underpinned Irish life and continue to shape it into the present. The series also aims to explore the construction and meaning of key concepts such as 'crime' and 'evil' and the impact of such concepts on the individual, society and the state. In doing so, the series will embrace but also cut across key aspects of political, legal, economic, social and cultural history and raise questions about the nature of Irish society over time in fruitful and novel ways.

1. Brian Hanley, *Republicanism, Crime and Paramilitary Policing in Ireland, 1916–2020.*

2. Aogán Mulcahy, *Crime and Conflict in Northern Ireland, 1920–2022.*

List of Figures and Tables

FIGURES

TABLES

Acknowledgements

In writing this book I have incurred many debts, and I am deeply grateful to those who have helped on this long journey. My warm thanks to: Richard Mc Mahon and Ciara Molloy, the series editors, for their support and encouragement; the publisher's anonymous reviewers for valuable suggestions; Deirdre Healy, Siniša Malešević, Niall Ó Dochartaigh and Ian O'Donnell, who gave predictably helpful and insightful feedback on earlier drafts; the staff at the Public Record Office of Northern Ireland in Belfast for assistance with archive material; Mary Collins, for gracious and much-needed help with the final manuscript; and to numerous others who, with friendship, support and sound advice, helped nudge the project along at different times and bring it to a conclusion, including: Déaglán Mulcahy, Alice Feldman, Sara O'Sullivan, Ingrid Holme, Graham Ellison, Kieran McEvoy, Steve Loyal and Tanja Singewald. The book was much improved for their generous assistance, and all remaining errors are mine alone.

Introduction

This book examines the dynamics of crime and conflict in Northern Ireland over the century since its establishment. Crime and the criminal justice system have been greatly affected by the contested nature of Northern Irish society and the political violence which has been such a prominent feature of its history. Yet, despite Northern Ireland's being synonymous with conflict, its rate of recorded crime and victimisation remains lower than that of many other European countries. Here I explore how the contours of crime have developed against a backdrop of political division and violence, and during different historical periods of stability, conflict and transition.

The main political divisions in Northern Ireland revolve around its constitutional status and the different positions held by unionists/loyalists and nationalists/ republicans over its legitimacy. In broad terms, and at the risk of giving these blocs a false coherence and understating internal divisions within them, unionists and loyalists (predominantly Protestant) favour main-taining Northern Ireland's union with Great Britain, while nationalists and republicans (predominantly Catholic) favour a united Ireland. Identities, however, are not immune to change, and internal and external factors alike can shape the nature of individuals' cultural affiliations and national aspirations. For example, an economically robust and politically inclusive Irish Republic may bolster calls for the re-unification of Ireland; the same conditions in Northern Ireland (or, indeed, in Britain) may help sustain its position within the United Kingdom.

Moreover, there is evidence that institutional changes arising from the peace process have led to significant 'identity innovation' in terms of how some individuals see themselves,[1] while other social and demographic changes have altered and eroded many of the historical divisions in Northern Ireland. When Northern Ireland was established, Protestants comprised two-thirds of the population, and Catholics one-third. Gradually this ratio has narrowed, and the 2021 census reported that for the first time in Northern Ireland there are now more people from a Catholic background (45.7 per cent) than a Protestant one (43.5 per cent).[2] The census also confirmed that the alignment between religious background and political identity is more nuanced and contingent than is often assumed: 32 per cent of the population described their political identity as 'British only', 29 per cent as 'Irish only', and 20 per cent as 'Northern Irish only'. Additionally, a substantial minority of Northern Ireland's population no longer characterise themselves as nationalist or unionist. For example, the 2021 Northern Ireland Life and Times Survey found that 32 per cent of respondents described themselves as 'unionist', 26 per cent as 'nationalist', and 38 per cent as 'neither'.[3] Cumulatively, the characterisation of Northern Ireland as a place of binary identities structured in a dominant/subordinate relationship has become glaringly less tenable.

Yet, even as the sands of identity shift, the fact remains that political divisions between unionist and nationalist communities have been the key axis of identity and conflict across Northern Ireland's history. That cleavage was the basis on which Northern Ireland was established, and it has underpinned social relations within it ever since, leading to the widespread violence that erupted in the late 1960s (known colloquially as the 'Troubles'), and shaping the peace process and political transition following the 1998 Belfast Agreement, which sought to resolve the conflict and establish a new beginning for Northern Ireland.

On that basis, conflict seems to be a fundamental feature of Northern Irish society, as evidenced by the violence accompanying Northern Ireland's creation, the three decades of the Troubles, and the fragile dynamics of the subsequent peace process. However, that is only part of the story, for this conflict sits in awkward juxtaposition with the peace and stability which has also been a prominent feature of Northern Ireland's history, perhaps exemplified by the relatively low crime rate which has characterised Northern Irish society both historically and to the present day. In that sense, Northern Ireland offers an example of a low-crime society with an intermittent history of widespread and sustained violence. This book examines these apparent contradictions by providing a sociological analysis of the nature and dynamics of crime in Northern Ireland from 1920 to 2022. It highlights the interplay between 'ordinary' crime, political violence and criminal justice policy – particularly in relation to policing, given its role and prominence – during periods of stability, conflict and transition.

The rationale for this book arises from several factors. First, this book is the first academic analysis of crime and justice in Northern Ireland extending over the century since its establishment. In 1990, John Whyte observed: 'it is quite possible that, in proportion to size, Northern Ireland is the most heavily researched area on earth'.[4] Certainly, while Northern Ireland has been the focus of a vast research literature, the knowledge this generated was deep but uneven. Much of that work has focused on the origins, dynamics and impact of the Northern Ireland conflict specifically, and that topic has deservedly commanded a great deal of researchers' attention. Whyte's observation, however, masks the reality that while the conflict has attracted vast amounts of attention, other issues – such as crime, and particularly the intersection between crime and conflict – have received much less.

Second, while Northern Ireland features prominently within the literature on 'divided societies' as a case study to highlight features of this political model,[5] in many ways it is atypical of the scale of challenges facing other societies. Looked at in the round, its contribution to debates about the dynamics of crime and its relationship with wider conflict in these contexts has been limited. Research on these issues has instead generally focused on sites of violence, war and upheaval far from the relative safety and stability of western Europe. Some important work on Northern Ireland has examined these issues in comparative settings, but again this focus tends to be on specific issues and across a limited timeframe.[6] This book seeks to address the dynamic between crime and conflict in a more sustained manner than has been done previously.

Third, the timeframe under analysis here provides an opportunity to consider the dynamics of crime and conflict across three discrete time periods and phases of Northern Ireland's socio-political history. Despite the understandable focus upon the period of the Troubles, the history of Northern Ireland is a history of stability[7] – with all its uncertainties and divisions – as well as conflict; and while the Troubles led to upheaval and devastation, the landscape of the criminal justice system has also been characterised by long periods of stasis. Moreover, the various initiatives and reforms to the criminal justice system emerging in the aftermath of the conflict provide several examples of innovative policy developments that warrant analysis. Given the various issues that have come to prominence at different points, and particularly the impact that developments in the political arena have had on Northern Irish society as a whole, this book focuses on the relationship between crime and conflict across three distinct periods: (1) the uneasy *stability* that existed from its establishment through to the outbreak of widespread disturbances in the late 1960s; (2) the *conflict* of the Troubles through to the 1994 paramilitary ceasefires and 1998 Belfast Agreement; and (3) the subsequent peace process, as these issues unfolded against a backdrop of political *transition*.

Disputes over the status of Northern Ireland are reflected in its nomenclature, and some terms such as 'Ulster', 'six counties' or 'statelet' carry wider political connotations and are often explicitly used either to support or undermine its legitimacy. Prominent political scientists have highlighted the terminological difficulties applying to Northern Ireland given its contested status and its establishment as a devolved entity rather than an independent state. O'Leary notes that 'The entity loosely called "the South" is a state; the entity loosely called "the North" is not; and it never has been ... the island does not consist of two states named Ireland and Northern Ireland'.[8] Whyte prefers the term 'region' to refer to the territory of Northern Ireland given its constitutional status.[9] Here I use the term 'state' as a convenient shorthand and to reflect widespread usage of that term in public and popular discourse.

The history of Northern Ireland also demonstrates the complexities attached to any discussion of crime. It highlights especially the challenges of distinguishing, conceptually and practically, between crime committed with different motivations and in pursuit of different goals. In 1981 Margaret Thatcher, then prime minister of the UK, dismissed the claims of paramilitary prisoners seeking recognition as being politically motivated (discussed further in Chapter 2), stating that 'There is no such thing as political murder, political bombing or political violence. There is only criminal murder, criminal bombing and criminal violence'.[10] While such a neat distinction has obvious political appeal, it reflects neither the substance nor the complexity of these issues. Clearly, all breaches of the criminal law are crimes by definition, but states themselves routinely distinguish between 'ordinary' crime unrelated to political goals and crimes specifically motivated by and in pursuit of political goals, whether described as 'terrorism' or in other ways. This distinction is evident in legislation targeting politically motivated activities, and by the specification of new legal procedures, police powers and penal regimes to address it. However, as Thatcher's comments demonstrate, the distinction (or lack thereof) drawn between crime and politics can be deeply uneven, highly contested and often contradictory. Criminal justice processes which are established through political means to address activities defined as in pursuit of 'political ends' in some way can also be accompanied by a rejection of such a motivation to avoid any hints of legitimacy. As McEvoy writes, 'A "political" trial does not necessarily result in recognition of a political prisoner.'[11]

In the context of Northern Ireland, we can apply the standard definition of crime – an intentional breach of the criminal law – to what is often colloquially termed *ordinary crime*, that is, crime unconnected to wider political or paramilitary activities and strategies. However, alongside this, we must also consider *politically motivated crime*: crime undertaken specifically to advance political goals, and often under the auspices of paramilitary organisations. Yet the boundary between these categories of ordinary and politically motivated crime is less clear-cut that is often assumed. For example, some crime reflects Northern Ireland's divisions but is not conducted with a specific political goal in mind, such as sectarian assaults on the perceived basis of the victim's religious/ethnic background. Similarly, while some paramilitary crimes are committed explicitly in pursuit of political goals, many others are committed for organisational/ personal goals – such as bank robberies carried out for organisational fundraising, violence inflicted on someone due to a personal grievance, or drug dealing engaged in for personal gain[12] – and distinguishing between these different motivations can be difficult, if not impossible. As the chief constable of the Police Service of Northern Ireland (PSNI) stated in 2006, 'It is very hard to judge what is paramilitary crime and ... what is ordinary crime being committed by paramilitaries for their own gain rather than the organisation's gain.'[13] We also have crimes undertaken by members of the security forces on an individual basis, as well as clandestine actions which are at face value illegal, but which are sanctioned at organisational or governmental level and where the perpetrators operate in conditions of near-total impunity. In addition to the question over the strict legality of particular actions, we have the further complicating factor of the legitimacy with which such behaviour is viewed. Thus, paramilitary prisoners who were imprisoned as 'ordinary' criminals protested at this categorisation up to the point of starving themselves to death; and some prisoners or their direct representatives stood for parliamentary election and won. Paramilitary organisations have also promoted themselves as fundamentally opposed to ordinary crime (even while engaging in it) and have provided often brutal quasi-policing measures to address crime in their localities. Bearing in mind these complexities, it seems reasonable and necessary to distinguish conceptually and substantively between 'ordinary crime' and 'politically motivated crime' even if this distinction is difficult to apply practically in all instances and some forms of crime defy easy positioning within it. Throughout this book I have sought to tease out the dynamics between these two categories of crime and to highlight the complexities surrounding the relationship between crime and conflict.

Criminological research on Northern Ireland

While the discipline of criminology has grown in scale and prominence across the island of Ireland in recent decades, this is in stark contrast to the relative neglect shown to issues of crime and justice prior to that. Rolston and Tomlinson described criminology as Ireland's 'absentee discipline', such was the low level of interest it received, a characterisation that applied both north and south.[14]

Within British criminological debates, Northern Ireland was largely 'ignored'.[15] Pease and Morrissey noted a range of issues suitable for comparative research, as well as some issues which warranted attention in their own right, including 'the State's techniques in controlling large numbers of people who do not recognise its legitimacy'.[16] While this should mean that '[t]he ferries to Belfast should be full of criminologists', they nevertheless concluded that comparative research across the different countries of the United Kingdom 'virtually does not exist'.[17] In their review of criminological research in the UK during the 1980s, Jefferson and Shapland highlighted the work of some scholars on different aspects of the penal system, policing, and how 'emergency' provisions shaped the nature of the criminal justice system. Yet, despite the significance of the issues raised by this body of research, it remained peripheral to mainstream British criminology: 'Ironically, Northern Ireland has been, simultaneously, absolutely central to developments in law and order, and, in research terms, highly marginal.'[18]

This omission has been a feature of even the most prominent criminological texts, such as early editions of the authoritative *Oxford Handbook of Criminology* (*OHC*). For example, in the third edition published in 2002, Downes and Morgan outlined the huge human and financial costs of the Northern Ireland conflict and stated that the 'negative effects on public trust in British political institutions have been incalculable', with several prominent miscarriages of justice generating 'the greatest twentieth-century crisis of confidence in the administration of justice in Great Britain'.[19] Nonetheless, Northern Ireland received only a few isolated mentions across almost 1,250 pages. Later editions of the *OHC* have given significantly more attention to Northern Ireland: the sixth edition, published in 2017, includes a chapter on 'transitional justice' in which Northern Ireland features prominently.[20] The establishment of the Institute of Criminology and Criminal Justice at Queen's University Belfast and the Transitional Justice Institute at the University of Ulster added considerable visibility, capacity and momentum to criminological research in Northern Ireland. However, the bipolar nature of Northern Ireland's presence within UK criminology – prominent in relation to some specific issues and extreme events, and largely absent otherwise – highlights the contingent factors that shape criminological knowledge.

Brewer et al. characterised their own efforts to provide a detailed assessment of crime in Ireland, north and south, as akin to cartographers seeking to 'remove the dragons' that filled those parts of maps where knowledge of the terrain was scant and the imagination instead filled in the gaps with monstrous creatures.[21] Certainly, there were notable gaps in knowledge on a wide variety of topics, and the impact of the Troubles on crime and criminal justice remained the predominant framework of analysis.[22] Contributions on Northern Ireland are now more commonplace in UK criminology texts,[23] but it is telling that two of the major works to address crime and the criminal justice system in Northern Ireland have focused on comparing Northern Ireland and the Irish Republic, rather than examining Northern Ireland within the context of developments and trends in the UK as a whole.[24]

Within work on Northern Ireland, several scholars initially highlighted the tension between the 'ordinary' criminal justice system and the 'emergency' measures introduced during the conflict, critiquing the normalisation of special powers, and the implications of developments in Northern Ireland for criminal justice systems elsewhere.[25] Gradually, more and more work appeared on different aspects of crime and criminal justice, some with an explicitly critical approach, some adopting a more administrative framework.[26] This highlighted the impact that political division and violence had on different forms of crime and responses to it, including work on prisons,[27] policing,[28] the dynamics of crime and victimisation,[29] responses to violence against women,[30] joyriding and youth crime,[31] as well as analyses of the criminal justice system in transition[32] as the peace process unfolded.

One of the most striking and enduring findings of criminological research in Northern Ireland is its comparatively low level of crime, despite its glaring political divisions and high levels of deprivation. The dissonance between media-fuelled images of a society collapsing into violent chaos and its frequently noted low crime rates prompts 'seemingly absurd contrasts':

> the most picturesque of English market towns, where there is a notable absence of both bomb and bullet, have levels of ordinary crime which exceed strife-torn Belfast. Working-class, inner-city neighbourhoods in Northern Irish cities, where social deprivation is very high, have lower levels of fear of crime than is found in other cities in Great Britain or the Irish Republic.[33]

Much of the literature on crime in Northern Ireland has highlighted this tension between political violence and low levels of 'ordinary' crime. Explanations for this apparent paradox have highlighted a combination of factors, particularly the conservativism, traditionalism and religiosity of Northern Irish society; the cohesion of community structures; high levels of surveillance and social control from state agencies and paramilitary organisations alike; and low levels of reporting and recording.[34] This research has, however, tended to approach the issue through the prism of the Troubles specifically or has been limited in its timeframe. None provides the historical overview that I seek to do here. Yet, the history of Northern Ireland is a history of stability – ironically – as well as overt conflict; and the landscape of the criminal justice system has been characterised by long periods of stasis as much as it has by sudden and dramatic change wrought by the onset of conflict or the transition to peace. By exploring these issues over an extended timeframe, this book seeks to add to our understanding of the relationship between crime and conflict in Northern Ireland.

Crime, conflict and political division

Extending our gaze beyond Northern Ireland, it is clear that the relationship between crime, political division and violence is complex and multi-faceted. Historically, these issues tended to be viewed as separate fields of inquiry, based in different disciplines, and operating with different theoretical frameworks, units of analysis and empirical foci. The fields of politics, international relations and law tended to hold sway over debates on war, political conflict, state security, human rights, transitional justice and related issues, while the emergent discipline of criminology took crime as its explicit focus. Within criminology, individual-level and meso-level analysis predominated as the discipline grew during the twentieth century. Positivism focused on the various factors associated with criminal behaviour, particularly at an individual level.

Sutherland's early definition of the discipline as 'the study of the making of laws, the breaking of laws, and reactions to the breaking of laws' captured the range of issues falling under the scope of criminology.[35] But despite the role of the state being plainly evident through the criminalisation process and social policies enacted in response to crime – both issues recognised by Sutherland as fundamental features of criminology – explaining patterns of criminal behaviour became the default empirical focus. Approaches that analysed individuals who committed crime, the patterns of their behaviour, or cultures which facilitated crime largely ruled the day.

As criminology developed as a discipline, the dominance of positivist approaches reflected in individual-level explanations and a therapeutic orientation ensured that issues of state received relatively little attention. As Matza memorably claimed, 'Among their most notable accomplishments, the criminological positivists succeeded in what would seem the impossible. They separated the study of crime from the workings and theory of the state.'[36] Even as other perspectives emerged – such as the Chicago School, subcultural approaches and labelling theory – the state remained largely absent from explanatory frameworks. Notwithstanding the earlier efforts of some scholars, the designation of the state as an empirical focus within criminology largely came about through the efforts of the broad perspective of critical criminology and its understanding of the state in terms of frameworks of power and conflict.[37] The work of 'conflict criminologists' and Marxist-oriented criminologists in North

America, as well as strands of critical criminology in Europe and elsewhere, problematised states and social elites as crucial topics of inquiry. This field of study highlighted the criminalisation process, corruption and abuse of power, and ideological dimensions of state authority.[38] Yet it left largely unaddressed the nature and dynamics of crime in societies in which the state was contested, in which large-scale political conflict or division was endemic, or in states presided over by authoritarian regimes.

McGarry and Walklate note that criminology and victimology 'have yet to address war in the substantive ways demonstrated by other disciplines'.[39] Gradually, however, criminology has begun to focus on the relationship between crime, conflict and the wider political environment, reflected in the growth of a 'criminology of war' subdiscipline.[40] For Jamieson, while criminology has paid only 'intermittent' attention to the relationship between crime and war, sustained conflict provides an opportunity to explore fundamental criminological questions in extreme and contested settings:

As an empirical area of study, war offers a dramatic example of massive violence and victimisation *in extremis*. It reveals the highly contingent nature of the definition of crime. War crimes and abuses involve both collective and individual human action. They are accomplished both by individual actors and through state action in concert with private and corporate actors. Wars and states of emergency usher in massive increases in social regulation, punishment and ideological control and new techniques of surveillance, and this often entails a corresponding derogation of civil and political rights. War and states of emergency are moments of transparency when ... processes of domination, exclusion and punishment become more visible.[41]

Even in societies where conflicts might not approach the full-scale destruction of war or where even to view them as warlike is itself highly contested, the issue of law and order and the behaviour of the police and other agencies can nevertheless highlight underlying social divisions in stark ways. Indeed, law and order itself can supplant an initial grievance to become the key dynamic of any violent conflict that ensues. Drawing on the example of policing and the 1960s civil rights movement in the USA, Wright observed how law and order became the prism through which the developing riots were experienced and understood:

> ... once a group experiences exclusion and has no effective way of communicating what is happening to those who are not affected, the police become a lightning conductor ... If all other avenues of trans-ethnic communication and cooperation are absent, the substance of inter-ethnic relations tends to revolve around the antagonistic axis of law and order.[42]

Two factors, especially, led to this greater attentiveness to the relationship between crime and conflict, what some have termed the 'crime–conflict nexus'.[43] First, it reflects an increased awareness of the *global context of crime and justice*, and particularly concerns over global inequalities, regional differences, transnational policy flows, and greater reflexivity surrounding the assumptions of early criminological frameworks.[44] The assumption that criminology was 'universalistic' in its outlook was exactly that: an assumption. The 'global south' and regions of embedded political division were prominent omissions from criminology's self-concept.[45] The stark reality is that the conditions which animated much of the development of criminology – the actions and motivations of individuals, the dynamics of specific cultures, and the day-to-day effectiveness of a fully functioning justice system, all within industrialised, western democratic societies with substantial social infrastructure – did not then and do not now reflect the lived realities of much of the world's population. In 2022, only 50.5 per cent of the world's population were living in fully functioning democracies. The remaining 49.5 per cent – approximately four billion people – were living under totalitarian or authoritarian regimes, in 'failed states' or 'developing democracies'.[46]

For this proportion of the world's population, the contested nature of the state they live in and the core divisions which fracture it are fundamental features of their lives, and conflicts and wars continue to shape the world in significant ways. There were fifty-six active conflicts globally in 2020.[47] The majority of these are intrastate, that is, conflicts occurring within a single state. A small number of wars (particularly those in Syria and

Afghanistan) account for most conflict-deaths globally in recent years, but violent conflict nevertheless is spread across many countries worldwide.

Second, the relationship between crime and conflict has begun to receive much more sustained attention through a greater recognition of the *challenges of providing day-to-day security in conflict-ridden or transitional societies* and the knock-on effects this has for political stability and economic recovery. In 1994 the United Nations Development Programme called for a paradigm shift in our understanding of security, proposing a new emphasis on 'human security'. In effect, it argued that equating security only with states and borders ignored a fundamental reality: 'The world can never be at peace unless people have security in their daily lives.'[48] Specifically, it called for security to be understood in terms of people rather than territory, arguing that development measures were likely to be seriously undermined unless they also addressed public safety and the day-to-day security concerns of the population. By arguing for development initiatives to encompass human security, it shone a light on the need for the police forces and criminal justice system in societies emerging from conflict and crisis to adhere to principles of good governance, accountability and human rights.[49] 'Security sector reform' emerged as a broad approach to develop 'democratic policing' in a variety of different contexts, including: as part of international assistance and economic aid programmes; from political transitions or regime change, including the break-up of the Soviet Union or the collapse of a dictatorship or authoritarian regime; or in the case of societies emerging from major conflicts or wars.[50] More recently, the United Nations reiterated the importance of safety and security through its 'Sustainable Development Goals' adopted in 2015 specifying that the international community should: 'Promote peaceful and inclusive societies for sustainable development, provide access to justice for all and build effective, accountable and inclusive institutions at all levels'.[51] Collectively, these various measures have enhanced the prominence of safety and security in debates about development, inequality and sustainability.[52]

The scale of difficulties experienced in 'divided societies', 'failing states' or 'developing societies' are typically of a different order to those in democratic or developed societies. Hinton and Newburn suggest that 'developing democracies' tend to be characterised by weak democratic institutions, widespread corruption, significant levels of poverty and inequality, high levels of crime and social instability, and low levels of police accountability and effectiveness.[53] Similarly, in 'weak or failing states' the state's ability to provide basic services to its citizens has greatly diminished if not 'largely disappeared', leaving a significant lacuna in terms of day-to-day security.[54] In such settings, Braithwaite argues that crime may constitute a 'cascade' phenomenon, initiating a series of knock-on consequences, all of which can erode people's levels of safety and security, and the stability and functioning of the society they live in.[55]

The dynamics of crime in conflict settings can take different forms. Perhaps most prominently, a conflict may *increase* crime levels in different ways. It can involve crime committed by the main protagonists as part of a military or paramilitary campaign against their enemies or the wider population, as well as crimes committed by the regime to fund its activities. Conflict situations can also facilitate crime by generating greater criminal opportunities as the attention of the police is absorbed by state security concerns and public order. Moreover, the conflict may lead to an expanded black market in illicit goods and services, with all the opportunities for white-collar crime that accompany this. Such crime committed in the shadow of the conflict can include smuggling, corruption, extortion and other activities.[56]

Crime may also be *suppressed* during conflicts. The group most likely to engage in crime – young males – may be employed in formal security roles or directly involved in the conflict in other ways, and thus not in a position to commit crime to the extent possible in other contexts. Even in authoritarian states where overt conflict is rare, regimes may seek to cement their control through stringent security measures including extensive surveillance mechanisms. Such measures may be introduced ostensibly to monitor political opponents and maintain the political *status quo* but may extend to the surveillance of daily life on a level far beyond what one might expect in a stable democratic society. For example, while the former East Germany (the DDR) was an authoritarian state, the fact that it was relatively stable for so long is substantially due to the coercive control it exercised. It operated a system of state surveillance that, in effect, monitored the entire population through a vast network of informants and other forms of intelligence-gathering.[57] The files of the Stasi, the state security police, accounted for well over 100 kilometres of shelf-space. Over 170,000 people worked as informants, and some suggestions put the figure at three times that or more. It is possible that formal and occasional informants comprised up to one tenth of the adult population. Such security measures inevitably suppressed crime levels, and in situations where non-state actors also operated systems of social control, opportunities for criminal activity were reduced even further. The surveillance of political opponents can also be accompanied by a state preoccupation with crime control, with low-level crime and disorder being targeted by the police as a contaminant or an ideological threat to the well-being of wider society, and for any embarrassment it may pose to the regime. Such patterns of policing were evident in the former Soviet Union, Nazi Germany and other societies.[58]

It is also worth noting that conflict may increase cohesion within groups. Communities may place a greater emphasis on internal solidarity, perhaps because of alienation from the state or wider society. In such circumstances, crime might also be suppressed, more through the inhibiting effect of high levels of informal surveillance than any road-to-Damascus conversion on an individual's part. When crime does arise, communities may place a greater emphasis on it being addressed locally through informal measures rather than being reported to the police and captured within the official crime figures.[59]

Furthermore, transitional periods as conflicts are re-solved may also affect crime levels. This clearly varies across societies and contexts, but the social changes her-alded by political transitions can often increase recorded crime in different ways.[60] The upheaval of a transitional process may lead to new criminal opportunities as, for example, criminal gangs may now be able to operate more freely with a reduction in levels of policing and sur-veillance. Other crimes may become more visible as con-flict-related violence wanes and other events replace it in news headlines and political debate. Social processes that had been underway but were obscured by the conflict - such as the growth of different youth subcultures, the greater availability of consumer items, or the growth of economic spheres that may be susceptible to corruption or corporate crime – may now become more evident. For example, examining homicide levels in forty-four coun-tries across a fifty-year period, LaFree and Tseloni found that 'countries moving from autocratic to transitional de-mocracies experienced a significant increase in homicide rates'.[61] Self-imposed restraints may also be jettisoned as community cohesion no longer carries such significance and the victims of crimes such as domestic violence may be more likely to report their victimisation, especially if the public's level of trust in the police increases. The continuation of violence even after peace agreements can reflect the substantive factors underpinning the conflict. The divisions that gave rise to the conflict persist, the actors who came to prominence through their use of violence may even be bolstered by their role in the peace process, weapons may be widely available along with cultural norms enabling their use, and dissident factions may believe political capital can be gained by using violence as a 'spoiler' tactic.[62] Cumulatively, therefore, and perhaps counter-intuitively, the advent of peace may be accompanied by an increase in recorded crime.[63] Furthermore, transitions can also affect crime debates through the question of how to respond to crimes committed as part of a conflict,[64] as well as through changes to the criminal justice system, whether via police reform,[65] restorative justice initiatives or other 'bottom-up' measures to make the criminal justice system more responsive.[66]

Chapter outline

The following chapters consider the relationship between crime and conflict in Northern Ireland. While I have tried to contain the substantive discussion in each chapter within a specific time period for chronological clarity, at times the discussion extends beyond that to enhance the coherence of the overall narrative and to provide for a more holistic overview as appropriate.

Chapter 1 considers the period 1920–68, highlighting the origins of the partition of Ireland and the violence that accompanied Northern Ireland's establishment and erupted sporadically in subsequent decades. It shows how the deep political divisions that marked it from the start generated an underlying anxiety that was reflected in security policies. Despite this political division – whether latent or manifest – high levels of social conservatism and political stability helped contribute to Northern Ireland's ironic reputation as a 'low crime' society. This chapter shows how these features of Northern Irish society developed up to the start of the conflict.

Chapter 2 examines the period 1969–98. The outbreak of widespread violence in 1968/9 and the emergence of paramilitary campaigns changed the dynamics of crime and the nature of the criminal justice system in far-reaching ways. The chapter explores the contours of the conflict and assesses the impact that the Troubles had on the nature and scale of crime during those decades. It discusses the relationship between 'ordinary' and paramilitary crime throughout the Troubles. It also considers the nature of responses to crime during the conflict and following the 1994 paramilitary ceasefires, including the challenges that the security situation posed for providing an effective policing service, and the measures that paramilitary organisations enacted to provide an 'alternative' justice system.

Chapter 3 focuses on the dynamics of crime and justice during the peace process, covering the period 1999–2022. The peace process from the mid-1990s onwards offered the prospect of an end to political violence and, with it, an opportunity to reshape the criminal justice system. The 1998 Belfast Agreement led to significant initiatives across the field of criminal justice, particularly in relation to the police reform programme outlined in the 1999 Patten Report as well as a wider review of the criminal justice system. The chapter assesses some of these measures and considers their significance and impact.

It also examines how issues of crime and victimisation unfolded within this transitional period. Lastly, it considers how these issues in turn were affected by debates over the role that communities should play within the justice system, and the legacy of the past.

The Conclusion summarises the main findings and considers their implications for our understanding of the dynamics of crime and conflict in Northern Ireland itself, as well as more generally.

While I hope this book advances our knowledge of the field of crime and conflict in Northern Ireland, it remains a 'concise' book and there are many issues – whether the dynamics of specific forms of crime, or the operation of different elements of the criminal justice system – that warrant much greater attention than I can afford them here. This should not be taken to imply that those issues are trivial or inconsequential; it reflects both the limits of my own expertise and the scope of this book to address them comprehensively here. I hope that any deficiencies will spur others to examine them and thereby add to our knowledge and help produce a more holistic account of the relationship between crime and conflict in Northern Ireland.

Chapter 1

Stability: 1920–68

The social and political dynamics of Northern Ireland

WHEN NORTHERN IRELAND was created, its rationale was straightforward: to provide a political solution of sorts for unionists who did not want to be included within an independent Ireland.[1] The background to this was the growing nationalist movement in Ireland during the 1800s and early 1900s, with different strands favouring greater autonomy or outright independence from the United Kingdom. The prospect of 'home rule' – where an Irish parliament would have some control over its domestic matters – was deeply contested, with unionists mobilising and threatening violence if it were enacted. Its imminent introduction was thwarted by the outbreak of the First World War and overtaken by the 1916 Easter Rising in Ireland. Although the rebellion was short-lived and limited in its military scope, it gave greater prominence to and generated greater support for independence, particularly following the execution of the rebellion's leaders. The 1918 general election saw a huge victory for the nationalist Sinn Féin political party, with its candidates winning 73 of the 105 seats in Ireland. The unionist population was concentrated in the north-east of Ireland and remained vehemently opposed to independence; and unionist politicians won the vast majority of seats in what would become Northern Ireland. Sinn Féin formed a parliament in Dublin following its electoral victory and declared Irish independence. This led to the 1919–21 War of Independence/Anglo-Irish War, and ultimately to the partition of Ireland. Partition was the preferred solution of no party, and instead emerged as an alternative to the threat of an escalated war between Britain and Ireland. It led to a civil war in the Free State between pro- and anti-treaty blocs (see below), and it also caused violent upheaval in Northern Ireland, especially in the immediate period of 1920–2.

The establishment of Northern Ireland was a protracted process. Under the Government of Ireland Act 1920, Ireland was partitioned into Northern Ireland and what became the Irish Free State (and later the Republic of Ireland); the 1921 Anglo-Irish Treaty provided for Northern Ireland to remain within the United Kingdom, which it duly did. From the outset, Northern Ireland was established specifically to protect unionism and unionists, and its size and boundaries reflected this imperative. Of the six counties it comprised, two had substantial Protestant majorities, two had small Protestant majorities, and two had small Catholic majorities.[2] This reflected the balancing act between being sufficiently large to be a sustainable political entity and yet sufficiently small to ensure a built-in and enduring unionist majority.

The partition of Ireland into Northern Ireland and the Free State may have provided an apparent solution to the seemingly irreconcilable differences between unionists and nationalists, but ultimately it accommodated rather than resolved those differences.[3] Within its borders, Northern Ireland contained a substantial unionist majority, comprising approximately two-thirds of the population, but unionists remained highly conscious of the presence of a disenchanted nationalist minority in their midst. While some acts of conciliation occurred, for the most part the broad Catholic community was viewed not as a minority group to be integrated, but rather as one whose allegiance to the goal of a united Ireland – or at least, the perceived lack of commitment, if not outright antipathy, to Northern Ireland – meant it was seen as a disloyal bloc, a threat to be managed and controlled. As such, the institutions of the state were inherently skewed towards unionism by virtue of their raison d'être, while discrimination in favour of unionists was widely practised in public-sector employment, housing allocation, the gerrymandering of local authorities, the security and the criminal justice system, and other sectors.[4] Due to its fragile foundations and the dynamics arising from its majority-rule political structure, O'Leary and McGarry described Northern Ireland as 'the paradigm case of state- and nation-building failure in western Europe'.[5] It was characterised, if not always by outright coercion, then certainly by an absence of consensus.[6] This manifested in two contrasting historical trends of conflict and stability.

The period 1920–2 was marked by widespread violence, including the Irish Republican Army's (IRA) campaign against the northern state which largely involved violence between its members and the police and security forces, as well as widespread inter-communal violence. The worst of the violence was centred in Belfast, which accounted for more than 90 per cent of security-related fatalities: political and sectarian violence accounted for 498 deaths in the city between July 1920 and October 1922.[7] The intensity of that violence exceeded even that witnessed at the height of the Troubles:

> In 1972, by far the worst year of the recent Troubles, 298 people died in Belfast as a direct result of the crisis. However, in the first six months of 1922 alone, 285 fatalities resulted from political and sectarian conflict in the city.[8]

While this violence echoed issues of state in so far as it reflected conflict over political allegiances, it also seeped into other aspects of daily life, such as the spheres of employment and residence. As Northern Ireland came into being, more than 10,000 people were expelled from their workplaces, while some 23,000 people were forced from their homes.[9] The scale of such events ensured that they were experienced as communal, and they fostered a deep sense of grievance and anxiety as they were embedded into collective memory. Moreover, even as this violence highlighted ongoing mistrust between the two main blocs in Northern Irish society, it also raised concerns over how security could be provided in day-to-day settings against such a contested political backdrop.

Even amidst such intense violence, some incidents still had the capacity to generate widespread outrage. In one particularly prominent episode in March 1922, gunmen entered the McMahon family home in Belfast late one night and shot dead five members of the family and a family employee. The McMahon murders became one of the most prominent episodes of this era, and the *Belfast Telegraph* newspaper described it at the time as 'the most terrible assassination that has yet stained the name of Belfast'.[10] There seems little doubt that these murders were in retaliation for the murder by the IRA of two special constables the previous day, and in that sense formed part of a wider pattern of political violence and sectarian killings. However, the 'shocking impact' of the McMahon massacre derived not so much from its status as the 'epitome of sectarian killing' but rather 'from the ways in which it violated the accepted conventions of that type of violence', including proportionality in terms of the number of victims and the level of violence inflicted on them.[11] The fact that the killers wore police uniforms gave the murders an especial notoriety. Despite the absence of conclusive proof that the perpetrators were indeed police officers, it seems unlikely that the murders could have been committed without some form of police involvement, direct or otherwise; indeed, the plausibility of police involvement is strengthened by numerous other instances of police misconduct in that period, and also by the fact that other police officers believed the perpetrators to be among their colleagues, to the extent of naming individuals in signed 'affidavits'.[12] Moreover, given the context of the time, it is possible that disguise was never the intention, and that if the perpetrators were police officers, one of their goals was to demonstrate to the wider Catholic community precisely how vulnerable it was. Wearing uniforms transformed the perpetrators from isolated killers into instruments of the state, and the murders were perceived as such.

By the end of 1922 levels of violence declined dramatically, partly because the Civil War in the Irish Free State drew the attention of the IRA away from Northern Ireland, and 'by 1923 it could be said that the region was at peace',[13] or at least relatively stable; Belfast experienced no further sectarian killings until 1933. However, the legacy of this period was profound, with Catholics bearing the brunt of the violence: 'Only 23 per cent of the population in Belfast, they accounted for 56 per cent of deaths, 73 per cent of workplace expulsions and 80 per cent of those displaced',[14] leading to its frequent depiction as a 'pogrom' against a vulnerable minority community. More recent analysis of the violence during this period suggests that the dynamics of the conflict were more nuanced, and that the greater number of casualties suffered by the Catholic population partly reflected their lesser power and resources rather than arising from a completely one-sided affair;[15] in effect, the conflict was 'unequal' but 'reciprocal'.[16] Nevertheless, the intensity and nature of the violence highlighted the varying vulnerability of Catholic and Protestant communities, contributing to further residential segregation and political polarisation. The violence also cast a shadow over policing for decades to follow.

As the political situation stabilised, the economy fell into rapid decline. The linen and shipbuilding industries – huge employers and key pillars of Northern Ireland's economy – were prominent casualties of this process. As the great depression shook the world economy, in Northern Ireland unemployment rates soared to more than a quarter of the workforce. In 1932, protests over 'relief' for the poor spilled over into riots during which the police shot dead several people. In the following years, sectarianism and inter-communal violence erupted once again. In 1933, the first sectarian murder since 1922 was committed (the victim was a Catholic publican) and widespread rioting occurred in 1935, resulting in the deaths of eight Protestants and five Catholics.[17] The advent of the Second World War brought greater attention to issues of security, with local defence forces and thousands of soldiers stationed there. Several German air-raids took place, during which approximately 900 people were killed, but otherwise Northern Ireland was relatively untouched by the ravages of war. The IRA conducted some limited activities during the war, and launched a further campaign from 1956 to '62, but this largely petered out due to a lack of support from the wider nationalist community. In calling an end to its campaign, the IRA bemoaned 'the attitude of the general public whose minds have been deliberately distracted from the supreme issue facing the Irish people – the unity and freedom of Ireland'.[18] Seventeen people were killed during the campaign, including eight IRA members and six Royal Ulster Constabulary (RUC) officers.

Notwithstanding these bouts of violence, the social and political landscape of Northern Ireland for much of these decades was characterised by 'a remarkable calm'.[19]

While this may appear at odds with the subsequent development of a sustained conflict from the late 1960s onwards, it reflects the simple fact that many 'divided societies' are not inevitably characterised by widespread violence. Rather, the domination that one group exerts over another may be so comprehensive – which McGarry and O'Leary termed 'hegemonic control'[20] – that society is largely characterised by the absence of any overt strife. In effect, domination generates and sustains a contrived stability. This pattern is a feature of many authoritarian regimes, and for a variety of reasons this was the pattern that developed for much of Northern Ireland's history.

First, for most of the twentieth century, unionism's demographic majority translated into straightforward political dominance. The nature of the parliamentary electoral system from the late 1920s onwards – single-seat constituencies in which candidates were elected on a first-past-the-post basis – was explicitly 'majority friendly'. Given the segregated nature of Northern Ireland, most parliamentary constituencies were 'safe' seats and incumbents were largely unassailable. Candidates in many constituencies were elected unopposed, such was the futility of political engagement when the electoral outcome was so predictable. In 1933, for example, thirty-three out of fifty-two parliamentary seats were uncontested, and local authority elections also had a high rate of uncontested seats.[21] With politics in Northern Ireland largely reduced to a numbers game, unionists dominated the political sphere. Northern Ireland's devolved parliament at

Stormont was ruled by a single-party government – the Official Unionist Party (later becoming the Ulster Unionist Party) – from its inception until 1972. With one exception in 1969, all cabinet members over this fifty-year period were Protestant and the overwhelming majority were members of the Orange Order, an avowedly anti-Catholic organisation. The only piece of legislation to originate from a nationalist politician over the lifetime of the Stormont parliament was the Wild Birds Protection Act (Northern Ireland) 1931.

Second, Northern Ireland's stability was sustained by a formidable security apparatus. In the 1920s especially, Northern Ireland was intensely focused on its security and, indeed, its very survival.[22] It had a much higher level of policing than other parts of the UK, some of this discrepancy reflecting the difficulties of receiving rapid support from other UK police forces. In 1924, there was one police officer for every 160 people in Northern Ireland, compared to ratios of 1:669 in England and Wales, and 1:751 in Scotland.[23] Northern Ireland's police force, the Royal Ulster Constabulary, was envisaged as a crucial means of maintaining the unionist character of the state.[24] It was supplemented by the Ulster Special Constabulary, a militia-style force that initially comprised three main branches (A, B and C), and in the 1920s 'close on one adult male Protestant in every five' was a member of the 'Specials'.[25] However, as the political environment stabilised and violence diminished, the A and C branches were phased out and only the B-Specials continued. The B-Specials served on a part-time basis (typically one evening per week or at weekends) and were largely used as an auxiliary security force. As the Hunt Committee noted, the focus of the B-Specials was 'almost wholly devoted to security duties of a military kind', including border patrols, guarding key installations and public order.[26] Widely viewed as a Protestant militia, it did not contain a *single* Catholic at the outbreak of the Troubles.[27] The B-Specials' local knowledge was a particularly valuable resource in monitoring and countering republican activity; they patrolled their local areas, and effectively they policed their Catholic neighbours; to the poet Seamus Heaney, they were 'neighbours on the road at night with guns'.[28] However, any gains from this intimate form of policing and surveillance had to be measured against the damage caused to community relations and state legitimacy: it elevated unionists above nationalists in terms of being entrusted with responsibility for security, with a predictably negative impact on community relations.[29]

In her anthropological study of social relations in Northern Ireland, Harris observed the importance that rural/border Protestant communities placed on the B-Specials. One Protestant woman 'spoke of them as if the existence of this organisation was vital to the continued existence of Protestants in her area'.[30] The ScarmanTribunal noted that Catholics viewed them in an entirely different light: 'Totally distrusted by Catholics, who saw them as the strong arm of the Protestant ascendancy, they could not show themselves in a Catholic area without heightening tension.'[31] Frequently mired in allegations of misconduct, it remained a controversial and polarising entity throughout its existence, and this was the basis on which the 1969 Hunt Committee recommended its disbandment.[32]

These personnel operated under permissive legislation, exemplified by the Civil Authorities (Special Powers) Act 1922. It gave the minister for home affairs the powers 'to take all such steps and issue all such orders as may be necessary for preserving the peace and maintaining order'. It included provisions for the imposition of the death penalty, as well as the prohibition of inquests, arrest without trial, the banning of demonstrations, and the destruction of buildings. It also included a striking 'catch-all' provision if the above powers were somehow found to be insufficient: 'If any person does any act of such a nature as to be calculated to be prejudicial to the preservation of the peace or maintenance of order in Northern Ireland and not specifically provided for in the regulations, he shall be deemed to be guilty of an offence under the regulations.' The act was renewed annually until 1928, when it was renewed for a five-year period, and in 1933 it was made permanent (it was eventually replaced in 1973 by the Emergency Provisions Act). The scope of the act so impressed the South African minister for justice that, when introducing a Coercion Bill in the South African parliament in 1963, he stated that he 'would be willing to exchange all the legislation of that sort for one clause of the Northern Ireland Special Powers Act'.[33]

Third, Northern Irish society was also characterised by moral conservatism and an abiding traditionalism. For example, homosexuality was decriminalised in England

and Wales in 1967, but remained criminalised in Northern Ireland until 1982. Furthermore, the circumstances under which an abortion was permitted in Northern Ireland were highly restrictive, and for decades the 1967 Abortion Act did not apply in Northern Ireland; only in 2019, with Northern Ireland's power-sharing executive suspended, did Westminster MPs vote to extend abortion rights in Northern Ireland.[34] Rates of religious identification and practice also were very high historically. In the 1961 Northern Ireland census, 'only 384 persons out of one and a half million identified themselves as atheists, free-thinkers or humanists',[35] approximately one in every 4,000 people. In 1968, 95 per cent of Catholics stated that they attended mass on a weekly basis (by 2003 this had dropped to 60 per cent). For Protestants in Northern Ireland, rates of church attendance are lower than for Catholics, but remain considerably higher than for Protestants in Britain. In total, approximately 57 per cent of Northern Ireland's population attended church at least monthly in 1999, compared to 13 per cent in Britain. In contrast, across nine western European countries, 30 per cent of the population in 1999 attended church once a month or more, a decline from 36 per cent in 1981.[36] As Mitchell, writing in 2006, noted, 'religious practices are deeply embedded in Northern Ireland', and 'whilst churchgoing in Northern Ireland has declined since the 1960s, it continues to be a thriving practice in comparison with many other western European states'.[37]

Against the backdrop of these socio-political factors, social interactions tended to follow established patterns. In many ways, as Akenson noted in his historical study of inter-group relations, only 'small differences' distinguished Irish Catholics from Irish Protestants, and it was the fact of this contrast rather than its scale which underpinned social relations.[38] These differences were strongly held but tended to play out in non-violent ways.[39] Rather, a prevalent set of stereotypes highlighted the distinctions drawn between 'your own' and the 'other sort':

> Protestants willingly contrasted their industriousness, cleanliness, loyalty to the crown, democratic ethos and freedom of religious expression with Catholic laziness, scruffiness, treachery, clannishness, high reproductive drives and priest domination. Catholics, for their part, spoke of Protestant bigotry, narrowmindedness, illogical clannishness, discrimination, individualism and money-centredness contrasting this with their own toleration, openness, community spirit and interest in 'culture' and the finer things in life.[40]

One might assume the outcome of such stereotyping was to exacerbate social divisions even further. Yet it is clear that 'the stereotyping is not all negative in tone',[41] and the use people made of such readily available scripts was often characterised by nuance and 'even an element of deep ambivalence' if not outright contradiction.[42] Akenson argues that while the Catholic and Protestant worldviews were 'myth making machines' that generated a bifurcated understanding of the world, they also functioned in practical terms as a cognitive map that provided a sense of one's own identity and that of others. The presence of such durable cosmologies bolstered each group's sense of certainty as to the nature of the society they inhabited, and thus solidified those social relations even further:

> ... each Irish group gave to the other adequate opportunities for fulsome self-love. In imaginatively calendaring the ways in which they differed, one from the other, in dwelling on details too minor to matter but too delicious to forget, they kept alive, by the great god of contrast, their own sharp and treasured self-definitions.[43]

In this way, social life was largely played out in complex systems of interaction which enabled 'certain people to live cheek by jowl with members of "the other side" and yet, without necessarily intending this, be socially quite isolated from them'.[44] Day-to-day relations could be entirely cordial, a veneer of politeness and sociability masking enduring stereotypes and often an underlying distance and mistrust. As Seamus Heaney observed in his 1975 poem 'Whatever You Say, Say Nothing', social relations were premised on the avoidance of many topics, on being 'Expertly civil-tongued with civil neighbours', with all of the intricate patterns of censorship, disclosure, circumspection and evasion that entailed: 'Smoke signals are loud-mouthed compared with us'.[45]

Ultimately, Catholic and Protestant communities lived largely separate from each other, segregated by housing, education, marriage[46] and employment; and while these patterns were not immune to change, they were remarkably enduring. This institutional estrangement was mirrored in day-to-day life through the deployment of a sophisticated diagnostic framework to ascribe religious identity to others: to 'tell'[47] members of one group from another and thus 'recognise the other side'.[48] While this communal homogeneity produced its own negative consequences in terms of heightened levels of segregation, it also ensured a degree of stability and cohesion.[49]

Crime and the criminal justice system

During the 1800s, Ireland was frequently characterised as a place of 'outrage' or 'disorder', but this was mainly in relation to violence associated with political protest, the inequities of land ownership, or intercommunal riots. In respect of ordinary crime in Belfast and the counties that would become Northern Ireland, levels of recorded crime were low and not an issue for serious public concern.[50] In the decades following the creation of the state, this pattern seems to have continued, and Bardon states that after the 'horrors of 1922', Northern Ireland enjoyed 'perhaps the lowest "ordinary" crime rate in Europe'.[51]

Figure 1.1 shows the level and rate of indictable offences (crimes that could be dealt with by judge and jury, and that comprised the standard way of publishing crime figures historically) recorded by the police from 1923

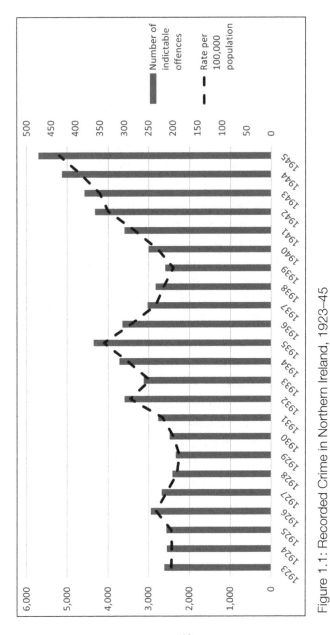

Figure 1.1: Recorded Crime in Northern Ireland, 1923–45

Source: Public Record Office of Northern Ireland (PRONI) files on criminal statistics (FIN/42/1, HA/4/2/536–542, and HA/5/1389).

to '45. The rate of crime doubled over this period, but it exceeded 300 offences per 100,000 population in only four of those twenty-three years, and it was less than 200 offences per 100,000 population in a further four years. It fell to its lowest level in 1929 when 187 offences per 100,000 population were recorded. This was equivalent, say, in a city of 100,000 people, to fifteen crimes being recorded by the police each month, or one crime every other day.

Archer and Gartner's painstaking comparative research supports the view that Northern Ireland's crime rate was distinctly and conspicuously low during this period (see Appendix).[52] Collecting data across many countries for a specified range of crimes, they considered several factors that might explain crime (and homicide rates in particular), including levels of urbanisation, upheaval arising from the aftermath of war, and so on. The data they present for Northern Ireland shows that once the violence of 1920–22 subsided (the number of homicides fell from 309 in 1922 to ten in 1923), homicide rates in the period 1923–45 exceeded one per 100,000 population on only four occasions. Researchers have documented a general historical decline in homicide rates in many western countries prior to the twentieth century,[53] but Northern Ireland stands out for its low homicide levels, nonetheless. Rape is a notoriously underreported crime, but the consistency in the number of reported rapes over this period is striking. On only three occasions were more than four rapes reported in any year over this period, and an average of 2.6 rapes were reported annually. The level of rapes was low even at the height of the violence and conflict surrounding the establishment of Northern Ireland; in 1922 Churchill described such crimes as 'of rare occurrence in Ireland'.[54] Clearly, that perception omits any consideration of the scale of unreported rapes, and instead is limited to comparison with levels of reported rape in other jurisdictions. Bearing in mind those limitations, overall rates of recorded crime for specific offences were considerably lower in Northern Ireland than in many other European countries. By comparison, France's recorded rates for murder and rape during the 1930s were approximately double and triple, respectively, those of Northern Ireland at the time.[55]

As a result of such low crime rates, many aspects of the criminal justice system generated little public interest or otherwise escaped scrutiny, including the treatment of young offenders. Prior to partition, all the institutions to detain young offenders were in the southern counties of Ireland. From 1921 to '26, over sixty boys sentenced to borstal were transferred to England, at which point a borstal wing was added to Malone Training School in Belfast to enable those concerned to be detained in Northern Ireland.[56] Youth subcultures clearly existed in Northern Ireland, but they were much less prominent than in Britain; and while youth crime was the subject of public debate from time to time, there was little equivalence to the moral panic surrounding mods and rockers and youth subcultures generally that was such a feature of British society in the 1960s.[57]

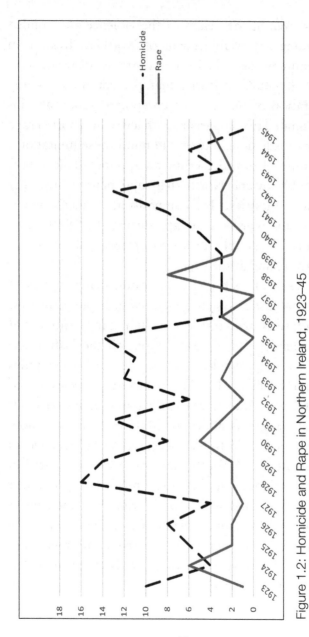

Figure 1.2: Homicide and Rape in Northern Ireland, 1923–45

Source: Dane Archer and Rosemary Gartner, *Violence and Crime in Cross-National Perspective* (New Haven, CT: Yale University Press, 1984), data appendix.

In respect of the penal system, while the authorities faced ongoing challenges arising from the imprisonment of politically motivated prisoners, Northern Ireland's low crime levels and 'gratifying respectability' ensured that its prison regime attracted little public attention. According to McConville, because Northern Ireland was 'a law-abiding part of the world, diligently observant in its religions, social control stiffened by family, community and locality, there was relatively little demand for prison services'.[58]

The use of internment – the detention of individuals without trial – at various points contributed to fluctuations in the size of the prison population, but overall levels of imprisonment were notably low. Northern Ireland's prison population was 329 in 1929, 361 in 1939, and 279 in 1950 (giving approximate imprisonment rates for these years, respectively, of 26, 28 and 20 per 100,000 population). This increased to about 350 during the early 1950s, and it increased further again over the following decade before declining to 403 by 1965. The daily prison population in 1969 was 483 (an imprisonment rate of 33 per 100,000 population), although that increased rapidly over the course of the year and beyond as levels of violence increased exponentially.[59] By the start of the conflict in 1969, Northern Ireland's prison population was 617, of whom nine were women.[60]

Probation too was an area of 'low priority' during these years.[61] In 1937 there were only ten probation officers for the whole of Northern Ireland. The service was almost entirely oriented to young offenders: less than one per cent of the probation orders issued related to individuals over twenty-one years of age. Probation orders were issued only in the larger towns and cities, and most of Northern Ireland's courts issued none whatsoever. Some of this reflects the 'notorious' failure of rural justices to fulfil their responsibility to appoint probation officers.[62] This might have reflected financial considerations, but it also signalled a certain scepticism towards the probation role: 'some justices undoubtedly thought that rural society and rural delinquent alike could survive without the probation officer'.[63] Overall, probation was 'sporadic, poorly funded and concentrated in Belfast', and even after the Ministry for Home Affairs took responsibility for probation from 1950 onwards, 'the number of people subject to probation supervision expanded but remained at relatively low levels'.[64]

While ordinary crime and the manner of its treatment within the criminal justice system were relatively uncontentious issues during these decades, the same could not be said for Northern Ireland's system of emergency legislation. Throughout Northern Ireland's history the Special Powers Act was an enduring source of concern. The manner in which it was used shifted from 'focusing on establishing order … to silencing support for union with the South', and 'the government soon heralded emergency legislation as essential to maintaining Northern Ireland's political institutions'.[65] 'Security' is, of course, both a material condition and a subjective perception, and the very potential of a threat underpinned unionist concerns. The Special Powers Act tended to be used less as the years passed, but its relentless renewal irrespective of levels of violence or the wider political environment conveyed an important symbolic message of the unionist government's vocal commitment to maintaining the security of the state, even when tangible threats against it were negligible or inchoate.[66] This symbolic issue may have eclipsed the more practical issue of its level of usage,[67] but regardless of whether this was the case, in its usage it was 'levied almost entirely' against the Catholic population.[68] As such, it remained a prominent source of grievance throughout its existence, and its repeal was one of the key demands of the civil rights movement that emerged in the 1960s.

Issues of state cast a long shadow over policing particularly, and shaped relations between the public and the RUC in fundamental ways. Unionist domination over the political sphere was enduring and near-total, and this ethos permeated both the RUC itself as well as institutions of government. McGarry and O'Leary observed that 'It would be astonishing if any police service could have preserved its autonomy from political interference given this level of political monopoly and continuity'.[69] One Catholic senior civil servant noted that the issue of loyalty was particularly significant in some postings: 'It was common knowledge that there were offices, the most [notable] being the Police Division in Home Affairs and the Cabinet Office, to which Catholics were not appointed.'[70] The subservice of the RUC to the unionist political establishment 'stunned' British politicians as the emergence of the civil rights movement brought wider public attention to these issues. One

Labour member of parliament recalled, 'The way the old Home Affairs department in Northern Ireland ran the police, my God, I mean the police were the creatures of the mini-aristocracy.'[71] Merlyn Rees, a Labour MP who served as secretary of state for Northern Ireland between 1974 and '76, noted the RUC's subordinate role: 'The stories one heard about the RUC inspectors. When one visited Fermanagh to see the Prime Minister Brooke, he had to go through the side door like a servant.'[72]

In any society, police–public relations are complex matters and it is important to recognise the significance of particular roles, activities and moments. Moreover, reality can be more contingent than strident positions may admit. Some commentators suggest that policing prior to the Troubles was largely a mundane affair. For example, John Hermon, who served as RUC chief constable from 1980 to '89, notes in his autobiography that when he joined the RUC in 1950, the highlights of his initial policing duties included cycling in 'hot pursuit' of an errant cyclist who was not using a light on his bicycle.[73] In another incident, the drama concerned a misunderstanding in which he wrongly accused someone of setting gorse bushes on fire, when in fact the individual concerned had spent considerable time trying to extinguish the fire. Such recollections of an innocent, bygone age are a familiar component of many police autobiographies, but in the context of Northern Ireland this focus on the minutiae of police life to the exclusion of the political backdrop reflects the wider characterisation of Northern Ireland as a place of stability and safety, in which the RUC's close knowledge of the community played a crucial role. In Ryder's view, 'If it had not been for the sectarian layer of affairs, the degree of public tranquillity in Ulster would have been unbeatable, thanks to the grass roots effectiveness of the RUC.'[74]

Harris suggests that attitudes to the police were somewhat more nuanced than is often assumed. For example, amongst the rural communities she studied she found that while there were clear differences in the broad outlook of Catholics and Protestants to the police, Catholic condemnation of the RUC and Protestant celebration of it was not always absolute: 'Catholics were particularly ready to damn the police and maintain that they favoured Protestants but few ordinary Protestants thought of the police as their especial friends.'[75] Nevertheless, in the decades prior to the Troubles, it seems clear that 'until 1968–9 the RUC enjoyed some grudging degree of acceptance among northern nationalists, if not republicans'.[76] McGarry and O'Leary state that 'when the RUC was confined to ordinary policing duties, interactions between the police and Catholics could often be civil'.[77] Whyte's careful analysis led him to conclude that the RUC was 'teetering uncertainly between impartiality and partisanship',[78] with a trend towards greater impartiality, until the outbreak of widespread violence in the late 1960s and criticism of police behaviour led to greater polarisation.

The RUC certainly enjoyed a better reputation among Catholics than the B-Specials did and in respect of non-political matters at least, it operated with substantial (if fluctuating) public support.[79] Normal policing prevailed in many day-to-day settings during periods of political calm, but security was a constant undertone. In one case in 1957, RUC officers stopped Frankie Meehan and asked him his name. When Meehan responded in Irish, he was arrested and detained without trial for seven months.[80] Ellison and Smyth also noted a constant tension between the RUC's 'ordinary' policing role, and the conflict that arose from its state security role. Thus, even during periods of IRA dormancy, RUC officers would 'keep an eye out – in a nice way mind you' on 'the politically motivated Catholic': 'Quite honestly the local IRA boys couldn't so much as fart and we'd get to know about it ... It was good crack [*sic*] in them days ... like you'd maybe pull a few boys in and give them a bit of grief ... the Specials would give them a bit of a rub over when they met them out one night.'[81] The emphasis upon security not only generated resentment from nationalists, it may also have undermined the RUC's role in crime prevention. For example, for much of the 1950s, Belfast was under-policed in respect of ordinary crime because of the relatively high proportion of police resources absorbed by state security duties.[82]

In terms of crime levels, in 1945 a total of 5,709 indictable offences were recorded in Northern Ireland, a rate of 433 offences per 100,000 population. Problematic relations with the police surely affected reporting rates in some areas but, given the relative political stability during these decades, it seems likely there was no great change in the propensity to report crime and so this would have had only a limited impact on the overall trajectory of

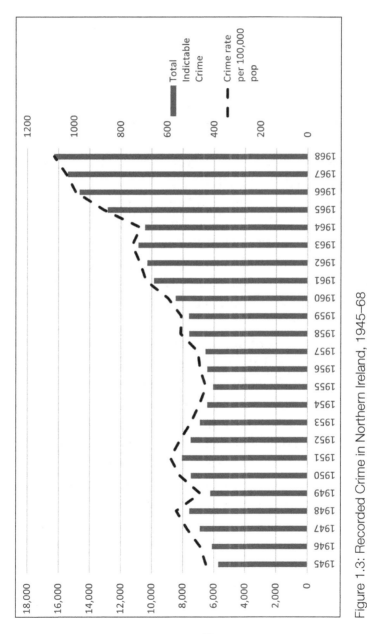

Figure 1.3: Recorded Crime in Northern Ireland, 1945–68

Source: John Brewer, Bill Lockhart and Paula Rodgers, *Crime in Ireland 1945–1995: Here be Dragons* (Oxford: Clarendon, 1997); and Northern Ireland Statistics and Research Agency.

recorded crime rates. Over the next two decades, crime levels rose gradually, particularly in the early 1960s, but the crime rate remained low generally. For example, in 1950 there were 546 offences per 100,000 population in Northern Ireland, compared to 1,094 offences per 100,000 population in England and Wales. From the mid-1960s on, the crime level and the crime rate both rose sharply (a similar pattern was evident in Ireland and in England and Wales, albeit with the notable increase in crime levels in England and Wales beginning a decade earlier[83]), while the detection rate declined to 29 per cent, just over a half of its 1945 figure of 55 per cent. By 1968, 16,292 indictable offences were recorded, a rate of 1,085 offences per 100,000 population – approximately three times the crime *level* and over twice the crime *rate* recorded in 1945.

In the absence of robust victimisation studies that might support or challenge the reliability of these data, it is difficult to offer definitive judgements on crime levels during this period. But the data are supported by much commentary on Northern Irish society over these decades which treats crime as no more than a minor factor in public debate, certainly when compared to the prominence attached to political developments.[84] Nationalist mistrust of the police might have affected reporting rates, but most observers suggest that the policing of ordinary (as opposed to politically motivated) crime was not a subject of major controversy, and thus the underlying political divisions are unlikely to have distorted the crime rates in fundamental ways. As elsewhere, most recorded crime was property-related, and levels of violent crime were extremely low. For example, in respect of homicide offences (murder and manslaughter combined), which are subject to least challenge on the grounds of accuracy and reporting/recording, the situation seems unambiguous. A total of sixteen homicides was recorded in 1960, but this was an anomaly arising from the IRA's border campaign and it did not reflect the broader pattern. Over the period 1945–68, three or fewer homicides were recorded in fifteen of those twenty-four years, and none were recorded on two occasions (1959 and 1963). This relatively pacific backdrop helped establish and solidify Northern Ireland's reputation as a low-crime society.[85]

As with the Irish Republic, however, allegations of the abuse of young people in a variety of religious and other institutions emerged in recent years, leading to the establishment of the Historical Institutional Abuse Inquiry to investigate allegations relating to the years 1922–55. The ten-volume report published in 2017 charted systemic failings across a range of institutional contexts, including physical and sexual abuse, neglect, and a failure in structures of governance and oversight that enabled such behaviour to continue for decades.[86] The characterisation of Northern Ireland as a low-crime society may be accurate in respect of levels of recorded crime, but as with other jurisdictions, the widespread institutional abuse suffered by young people is absent from that narrative, and any overall assessment of crime during this period must be tempered by the omission of events that proved so damaging to so many.[87]

Although the IRA's 1956–62 border campaign had been an abject failure in terms of generating nationalists' support, a few years later the underlying divisions within Northern Ireland resurfaced again. In 1964, the Campaign for Social Justice was established to protest at systematic discrimination against Catholics and nationalists, particularly in respect of public-sector jobs, housing allocation and the gerrymandering of electoral wards. Within this context, the Northern Ireland Civil Rights Association emerged in 1966. It became increasingly prominent and vocal in its campaign, arousing suspicion and hostility among unionists, and generating a violent backlash.[88] The first three victims of the conflict were killed by loyalists in 1966.[89] In 1968, a civil rights march on 5 October in Derry was baton-charged by RUC officers, television coverage of which was broadcast worldwide. Against a backdrop of growing political division and volatility, the Northern Irish prime minister sought to deliver a reform programme, but this satisfied neither nationalists who considered it too little, nor unionists who considered it too extensive.

By mid-1969, amidst protest and counter-protest, major rioting had broken out in Derry and Belfast. The security forces were too few in number and lacked the training and equipment necessary to contain the deteriorating situation. Misconduct by some members of the RUC and B-Specials greatly exacerbated matters, and while the 1969 Cameron Inquiry and 1972 Scarman Tribunal examined a variety of issues surrounding the emerging crisis, Scarman noted that 'In a very real sense our inquiry was an investigation of police misconduct'.[90] Both reports documented a spectrum of police misconduct, including 'unauthorised and irregular use of batons', indiscriminate use of water cannon on members of the public for which there was 'neither reason nor excuse', 'assault and battery, malicious damage to property ... use of provocative sectarian and political slogans ... [and] serious allegations of assaults'.[91] Scarman particularly highlighted the RUC's 'failure to prevent Protestant mobs from burning down Catholic houses' and the 'failure to take any effective action to restrain or disperse mobs or to protect lives and property' in riot areas.[92] Ultimately, Scarman credited the police response to the civil rights movement with creating what he gravely termed 'the fateful split between the Catholic community and the police'.[93] Amidst rising levels of violence, the Northern Ireland government was no longer able to maintain order and the British Army was deployed 'in aid of the civil power'. The Troubles had begun.

Chapter 2

Conflict: 1969–98

The contours of the conflict

THE WIDESPREAD VIOLENCE that erupted in Northern Ireland from late 1968 onwards was in stark contrast to the uneasy calm that prevailed during much of its history. Even though the events surrounding the civil rights movement amounted to a social and political earthquake, few would have predicted the scale and longevity of the conflict that would follow. In terms of measuring its impact, given the different criteria used by different sources and the disputed and ambiguous nature of various incidents, there are some differences in the figures compiled in various studies on the scale of the conflict (see Appendix). The longest continuous database is that compiled by the police, although this only includes deaths that occurred within Northern Ireland, whereas other sources include deaths from outside Northern Ireland. Police figures indicate that between 1969 and 2022, some 3,404 people died as a result of the conflict, while approximately 48,000 people were injured. For the period 1969–98 specifically, police data indicate 3,289 conflict-related deaths within Northern Ireland. The Sutton[1] database gives a total of 3,532 deaths for the period 1969–2001, and Melaugh's work to extend this indicates a further seventy-two deaths from 2002 to '22 (3,604 deaths in total, with an additional twenty-six deaths where it was unclear whether they were conflict-related).[2] McKittrick et al. document 3,717 deaths in the period 1969–2006 (with an additional three conflict-related deaths in 1966).[3] Sutton and McKittrick et al. estimate, respectively, that conflict-related deaths outside of Northern Ireland amounted to totals of 259 and 267.[4]

When we look at the annual figures, the intensity of the conflict in the early 1970s is fully apparent. Between 1962 and 1968 inclusive, an average of 2.7 homicides was recorded each year. As Figure 2.1 shows, the conflict led to a sudden and unparalleled increase in violent deaths (the following discussion draws on Sutton's work given its availability and ease of use). In 1969, sixteen people died as part of the conflict; this increased thirty-fold in three years, to an all-time high of 480 violent deaths in 1972 (ninety-five people were killed in July alone). The number of deaths dropped in subsequent years to an annual average of 276.5 deaths from 1973 to '76, and thereafter it dropped significantly again. The staggering increase in homicide levels is highlighted by Rose who, writing in 1976, observed that 'Not a single murder was reported in Northern Ireland in 1963, and only one each in 1964 and 1965. Since 1971, more often than not a killing has occurred each day'.[5] About half of all conflict-related deaths occurred in the years 1971–6; in only five subsequent years did the annual number of deaths exceed 100, and the last such occurrence was 1988.

While euphemistically termed the 'Troubles', 'in its duration and intensity relative to population size, the conflict approaches that of a war rather than a local insurgency'.[6] Extrapolating the number of fatalities to other societies gives a sense of the scale of the violence. In Britain, a comparable scale of conflict would have seen

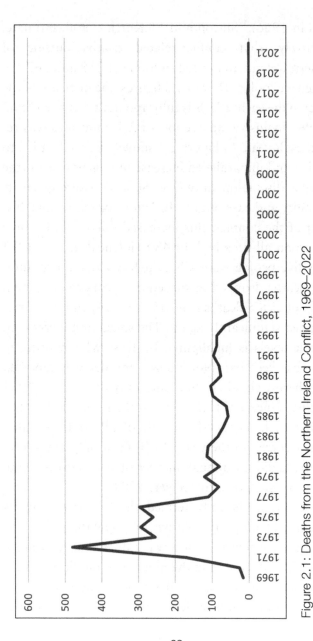

Figure 2.1: Deaths from the Northern Ireland Conflict, 1969–2022

Source: Malcolm Sutton, *An Index of Deaths from the Conflict in Northern Ireland* (2001), extended by Martin Melaugh for the period 2002–22, available at: https://cain.ulster.ac.uk/sutton/index.html. Melaugh lists a further twenty-six deaths over the period 2002–22 in which it was uncertain whether or not these were conflict-related.

approximately 126,000 people killed, just under half of Britain's death toll from the Second World War.[7] In the USA, a conflict of Northern Ireland's scale would have seen over 600,000 deaths, comparable to the number killed in the American Civil War, and approximately 50 per cent more than were killed during the Second World War, and nine times the number of Americans killed in the Vietnam War. Care is needed when engaging in any form of international comparison, and the specificities of each context are crucial. In Northern Ireland, these casualties occurred over a thirty-odd-year period and the violence was most intense in the early 1970s; and while the figures are high, they are certainly not unprecedented.[8] Nevertheless, for a population that averaged approximately 1.6 million people over the course of the Troubles, the conflict exacted a huge toll, and exposure (direct or indirect) to violence was widespread. In 1976, Rose estimated that 'nearly one family in every six has had a father, a son, a nephew or an aunt killed or injured in the Troubles'.[9] By the end of the conflict, one 1998 survey found that 14 per cent of respondents indicated they were a victim of a violent incident, 25 per cent had been caught up in an explosion, 56 per cent knew someone who was killed or injured in the conflict,[10] while 21 per cent had a family member or friend who had been killed or injured.[11]

Throughout the conflict, deaths were concentrated disproportionately in several areas. Belfast, Derry, the area of east Tyrone and north Armagh, and some border areas all had particularly high fatality levels, and there was a high correlation between levels of deprivation and fatality rates.[12] McKittrick et al.[13] estimate that almost half (49 per cent) of conflict-related deaths in Northern Ireland occurred in Belfast (most of these in north and west Belfast, and close to the city centre), and over half of Belfast's killings took place in 'only 3.8 percent' of its total area.[14]

One effect of the conflict, particularly in the early years, was to increase segregation levels as individuals sought the sanctuary of 'heartland' areas where their co-religionists were in a majority.[15] Indeed, the scale of people displaced through violence in Belfast in 1969 comprised what was then the largest forced displacement of people in Europe since the end of the Second World War.[16] Such residential patterns proved enduring: the 1991 census showed that 'half of Northern Ireland's population now lives in wards which are more than 90 percent Protestant or 90 percent Catholic'.[17] Ultimately, though, this had a mixed effect on people's vulnerability. Patterns of conflict reflected efforts to assert territorial control, and 'interfaces' were often the focal points for conflict in some contexts, while 'heartland' areas also featured high levels of violence in other contexts such as conflict between the British Army and republicans in the largely Catholic areas of west Belfast.[18] In addition to damaging 'the whole fabric' of the state and its civic culture, the impact of the conflict seeped down into the very core of community life:

religiously homogenous communities of defence emerged as a result of a vast process of resettlement, valued social relationships were ruptured, community trust was destroyed by government and paramilitary informants, the erection of social and physical barriers broke long established patterns of communal life, open communities were turned into closed ones.[19]

In terms of casualties and protagonists, Sutton's analysis indicates that just over half (1,841) of the victims were civilians. Of civilians killed within Northern Ireland, 1,099 were Catholic and 568 were Protestant. Just under a third of the total casualties were members of the security forces, and a further 16 per cent were paramilitaries (both republican and loyalist).

Status of the Victim	Number of Deaths	%
Civilian	1,841	52.1
Republican Paramilitary	396	11.2
Loyalist Paramilitary	170	4.8
British Security	1,114	31.5
Irish Security	11	0.3
Total	3,532	99.9

Table 2.1: Conflict-Related Deaths – Status of the Victim
Source: Malcolm Sutton, *An Index of Deaths from the Northern Ireland Conflict* (2001), available at: https://cain.ulster.ac.uk/sutton/index.

In terms of the organisation responsible, the vast majority of people killed died at the hands of paramilitaries. A total of 2,058 people were the victims of republican paramilitaries, and the vast majority (about 83 per cent) of these were killed by the IRA. Loyalist paramilitaries (especially the Ulster Volunteer Force and the Ulster Defence Association/Ulster Freedom Fighters) killed a total of 1,027 people.[20] The security forces were responsible for 370 deaths, including 299 by the British Army, and fifty-five by the RUC; five people were killed by the Irish security forces. In seventy-seven cases, the perpetrator was unknown.

Organisation responsible	Number of Deaths	%
British Security	365	10
Irish Security	5	0.1
Republican Paramilitaries	2,058	58
Loyalist Paramilitaries	1,027	29
Unknown	77	2
Total	3,532	99.1

Table 2.2 Conflict-Related Deaths – Organisation Responsible
Source: Malcolm Sutton, *An Index of Deaths from the Northern Ireland Conflict* (2001), available at: https://cain.ulster.ac.uk/sutton/index.

As the conflict surged in the early 1970s and levels of violence increased exponentially, the complexion of the criminal justice system transformed as it expanded to cope with huge increases in the number of people being charged, convicted and imprisoned. Between 1969 and 1998, there were 35,669 shootings, 10,142 explosions (equivalent to almost one explosion every single day over that period) with a further 5,104 explosive devices defused, and 20,568 armed robberies.[21] The prison population grew to just over 3,000 in late 1977 – a six-fold increase in eight years, reaching an imprisonment rate of just under 200 per 100,000 population – before gradually declining to under 2,000 prisoners by 1987 and to a low of 910 in 2001.[22] Throughout the Troubles, a large proportion of prisoners were members of paramilitary organisations and convicted of conflict-related offences – fluctuating between 50 per cent and 66 per cent of the overall prison population at different points.[23] The profile of the prison population changed from predominantly comprising 'ordinary' criminals to having a majority of paramilitary prisoners, many of whom were serving long-term or life sentences: 'Between 1973 and 1983, 440 men were committed to prison with life sentences. By 1987, lifers made up 28 percent of sentenced prisoners and about 40 percent of all the loyalist and republican political prisoners.'[24]

The growing prison population was far beyond what the penal system was designed to handle, causing significant challenges for inmates and staff alike: 'A prison system which was built to house just 600 prisoners managed by 292 staff in 1969 was forced to accommodate 2,687 prisoners by 1975 managed by 2,184 staff. In such circumstances, the physical realities of the prison estate as well as staff shortages severely limited the authorities' ability to do [anything] other than contain paramilitary prisoners.'[25] Male paramilitary prisoners were housed in the Maze Prison, site of the Long Kesh internment camp and also known as the 'H-Blocks' because of the distinctive shape of the structures. Female prisoners were housed in Armagh Gaol until 1986, thereafter in a unit within Maghaberry Prison, and more recently in Ash House, a unit within the Hydebank Wood Young Offenders Centre. In the Maze Prison, inmates were segregated into different blocks based on organisational affiliation and were afforded considerable autonomy in what was a highly distinctive prison regime. Unsurprisingly, the management of paramilitary prisoners was one of the key challenges facing the prison authorities, and the complexion of the prison population ensured that security concerns shaped the entire penal system. One Inspector of Prisons report noted the challenges this posed:

> They were quite unlike the population of any other prison in England or Wales in their dangerousness, their allegiance to a paramilitary organization, their cohesiveness, their common determination to escape and their resistance to the efforts of the prison authorities to treat them as ordinary criminals.[26]

Between 1974 and 1993, twenty-nine prison officers were killed, twenty-seven by republican paramilitaries and two by loyalist paramilitaries.[27]

Within the fields of security, the justice system and other state services, the risks faced by different professional groups were uneven. While soldiers, police and prison officers were repeatedly and aggressively targeted by paramilitaries, probation officers and social workers generally were not.[28] This situation arose because of the welfarist role they played and their adoption of a stance of 'neutrality' by voting in the 1970s to refuse to engage in mandatory supervision of politically motivated offenders. If this partly was to distance the probation service from being seen as a 'legitimate target', it also reflected the inherent professional difficulties of trying to 'rehabilitate' individuals who argued that their crimes reflected their commitment to their community rather than their alienation from it. While this stance softened when the issue of resettlement (as opposed to rehabilitation) of long-term paramilitary prisoners emerged in the 1980s, its neutrality stance nevertheless enabled probation officers to pull off 'a remarkable feat': 'Whilst other criminal justice personnel were targeted as enemies, probation officers were engaging directly in some of the most politicised and socially-excluded neighbourhoods.'[29]

It is difficult to be definitive in terms of the total number of people imprisoned due to the conflict, particularly in its early years, but it is in the order of 25,000–30,000 people – including 15,000 republican prisoners and between 5,000 and 10,000 loyalists.[30] A further 2,000 people were interned (detained without trial on suspicion of engaging in political violence) between 1971 and 1975. About 19,600 people were convicted of scheduled offences (those included on a 'schedule' or list of offences presumed to be linked to political violence) over the course of the conflict,[31] although that omits many people convicted in the early 1970s and internees. It is also important to realise that the experience of paramilitary imprisonment was relatively common in republican and loyalist communities in particular; one 2010 study by Jamieson and colleagues estimated that 'ex-political prisoners make up at least 13.5% of the male cohort of 50- to 59-year-olds in Northern Ireland'.[32] By the end of the conflict, about half of the prison population comprised individuals convicted of, or awaiting trial for, politically motivated offences.[33]

During the early 1970s, the British Army played the predominant role in maintaining security, and a range of highly contentious 'emergency' measures were put in place then, including the use of internment without trial. In time, some of these measures were phased out or replaced: the use of the army in some operations – such as in Ballymurphy in Belfast in 1971, in which British soldiers shot dead ten people, or Bloody Sunday in Derry in 1972, in which thirteen people were shot dead (with another man who was shot dying some months later) – was nothing short of disastrous.[34] Overall, though, the expansion of coercive powers available to the state, coupled with the huge increase in the number of security force personnel and the abrasive nature of the tactics being used (including widespread stop-and-search, equivalent to the 'mass screening' of entire areas) generated much criticism. It seemed that the rule of law associated with western liberal democracies was being undermined, and in effect replaced by a system underpinned by emergency powers, the erosion of constitutional safeguards, and the absence of any effective mechanisms of accountability or redress.[35]

The 1973 Diplock Commission considered changes to the administration of justice and recommended the establishment of jury-less courts for scheduled offences. Although the suspension of jury trials in such cases was based on concerns about jury intimidation and 'perverse acquittals', scant evidence was provided showing this to be a major problem, and the empirical basis for the introduction of 'Diplock courts' was 'astonishingly weak'.[36] Levels of public confidence in the criminal justice system reflected these concerns. One 1974 study, for example, found that 88 per cent of Catholics believed that 'a person does not get a fair trial in Northern Ireland', compared to 27 per cent of Protestants.[37] The weight of these changes to the criminal justice system was explicitly to enhance its effectiveness in addressing paramilitary activities. In the face of widespread criticism of this expansion of state power and its implications for the rule of law, judges were conscious of the need to emphasise their independence from government and their willingness to uphold defendants' rights. They presided over the Diplock court system, but they also demonstrated their willingness to acquit paramilitary defendants in various cases:[38] they 'may not have been steadfast champions of human rights, neither were they pliant servants of the State'.[39] Nevertheless, republican paramilitaries carried out at least eighteen attacks against members of the judiciary, including killing several magistrates, judges and their family members.[40]

In the mid-1970s, with no immediate prospect of the violence abating and no political solution in sight, the

British government implemented a new conflict management strategy of 'criminalisation'. This involved a major discursive shift in how the conflict would be framed and addressed. It was premised on reducing overt reliance on emergency measures and instead using the ordinary criminal justice system, albeit one fortified with greatly enhanced powers, including an expansion of the powers of arrest for members of the security forces and changes to the rules of evidence in criminal cases. It also involved a policy of 'police primacy' whereby the RUC replaced the army as the agency with primary responsibility for maintaining law and order, resulting in a huge expansion in the strength of the police force,[41] as well as changes in training and equipment to increase its effectiveness in dealing with paramilitary violence and public order situations.

Within the penal system, it meant the ending of internment, and the withdrawal of 'special category status' to paramilitary prisoners. Special category status had been introduced in 1972 and, in broad terms, it entailed prisoners convicted of conflict-related offences being granted the privileges previously available only to internees. By February 1976, some 1,476 prisoners (895 republicans and 581 loyalists) were imprisoned under this model, which mirrored 'prisoner-of-war' regimes much more closely than standard prison regimes to house convicted criminals. As Beresford described it:

The inmates – whether Republican or Loyalist – lived in dormitories in Nissen huts, segregated according to paramilitary allegiance. They organised and disciplined themselves with military-style command structures, drilled – with dummy guns made with woodworking equipment supplied by the prison – and held lectures on revolutionary politics and guerrilla warfare.[42]

The British government established the Gardiner Committee to review different aspects of the criminal justice system, including the detention of paramilitary prisoners. Describing some features of the 'prison situation' as 'appalling', it called the introduction of special category status 'a serious mistake' for the way it acknowledged the political motivation of paramilitary prisoners and thereby accorded them a degree of legitimacy:

We can see no justification for granting privileges to a large number of criminals convicted of very serious crimes, in many cases murder, merely because they claim political motivation. It supports their own view, which society must reject, that their political motivation in some way justifies their crimes.[43]

The report recommended that special category status be ended, and henceforth no new prisoners would be granted it. Paramilitary suspects now would be prosecuted through the jury-less Diplock courts with convictions increasingly obtained through confessions. The number of complaints of ill-treatment increased from 180 in 1975 to 671 in 1977, leading to a highly critical Amnesty International report and a commission of inquiry established by the British government.[44] Prisoners would now serve their sentences as 'ordinary criminals' in the Maze Prison rather than as special category prisoners in the internment compounds.

The characterisation of the conflict in these law-and-order terms generated a furious response from paramilitary prisoners, who viewed themselves explicitly as political prisoners and combatants rather than ordinary criminals.[45] Over the following years, many of them refused to wear prison uniforms and wore blankets instead (the 'blanket protest'), and did not leave their cells, smearing their excrement on the cell walls (the 'dirty protest'). Prisoner protests culminated in the 1980 and 1981 hunger strikes, during which ten republican prisoners starved themselves to death in protest at their designation as common criminals and in pursuit of what was effectively political prisoner status. Ironically, the election of several prisoners to the British and Irish parliaments helped convince the republican movement to increase its commitment to a strategy of electoral politics, even if strands of this approach were already in place during the 1970s.[46]

Throughout the 1980s, various political initiatives were attempted, including the 1985 Anglo-Irish Agreement, but while these shifted the dynamics of the political field in various ways, the conflict persisted.[47] In the early 1990s, however, there were signs of a political thaw. The Downing Street Declaration of December 1993 from the British and Irish governments was followed by an IRA ceasefire in August 1994, and by a loyalist ceasefire in October of that year. Amidst widespread euphoria that the conflict was finally over, it quickly became clear that more difficulties lay ahead. Political progress was painfully slow, the IRA ended its ceasefire (which it subsequently reinstated) with a massive bomb in London's Canary Wharf, and disputes over parades led to Northern Ireland's worst mass disturbances since the 1981 hunger strikes. Further political negotiations led to the 1998 Belfast Agreement, which seemed to lay the basis for a comprehensive settlement to the conflict, although subsequent events would demonstrate just how fragile was the peace.

Crime and victimisation

Against the above backdrop, let us now turn to *levels* of recorded crime during the conflict. As the conflict escalated in its early years, several official commentators anticipated that political violence would have a contagion effect. By destroying the social fabric, it would undermine the moral outlook of young people especially, sunder their social bonds, brutalise them, and increase their likelihood of engaging in crime.[48] Certainly, crime levels did rise markedly, but from a low initial base and to levels that remained relatively low compared to other societies; and the conflict likely inhibited crime in some ways too.

As the Troubles developed, official crime statistics included all recorded crimes, whether conflict-related or not. Additional data on 'security situation statistics' were published to document the crimes specifically arising from the conflict, typically comprised of 'scheduled offences' – those listed on a schedule of offences considered related to political violence (e.g. fire-arms and explosives offences).[49] Between 1968 and 1971, the number of offences recorded by the police almost doubled and increased more than threefold (to 54,262 offences) by 1979 (see Figure 2.2). During the 1980s and 1990s, recorded crime levels fluctuated somewhat and in 1994, the year of the paramilitary ceasefires, 67,886 offences were recorded. This dropped to 59,922 in 1997/8 (when reporting changed from a calendar-year basis to a financial-year basis), before rising to 76,644 offences in 1998/9, an increase of almost 28 per cent. Matters were further complicated by a change to recording practices in 1998 (the introduction of 'new counting rules', discussed further below) which saw the 1998/9 crime level under the new rules reach 109,053 offences. If we consider crime *rates*, in 1968 just under eleven offences per 1,000 population were recorded. This almost doubled by 1971, and it trebled by the late 1970s. It reached thirty-five offences per 1,000 population in 1979, and it did not fall below that rate again. In 1997/8, the crime rate was thirty-six offences per 1,000 population, rising to forty-six the following year under the 'old' counting rules, but to sixty-five offences per 1,000 population under the 'new' rules.

It is difficult in some instances to distinguish between deaths arising from the conflict and those unrelated to it, but based on a comparison of Sutton's data with police figures, Brewer et al. cautiously suggest that over the period 1969–93, no more than thirty murders *unrelated* to the Troubles took place in any given year (and in

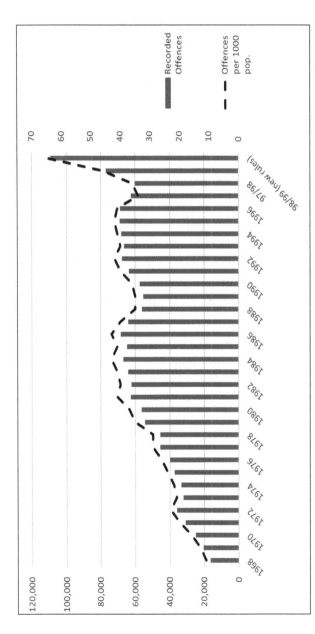

Figure 2.2: Recorded Crime in Northern Ireland, 1968–1998/9

Source: John Brewer, Bill Lockhart and Paula Rodgers, *Crime in Ireland 1945–1995: Here be Dragons* (Oxford: Clarendon, 1997), and PSNI.

Note that crime recording changed from a calendar year to a financial year basis in 1997, and a new system of recording crime (the 'counting rules') was established on 1 April 1998. The two sets of figures for 1998/9 include those generated under the 'old' rules (in place up until 31 March 1998) as well as under the 'new' rules.

one year, 1990, there were none).[50] Overall, they estimate an annual average of thirteen murders unrelated to the conflict (slightly over 0.8 per 100,000 population for this period). Bearing in mind the extremely low homicide levels historically, this nevertheless represents a significant increase since the decades prior to the Troubles (see Appendix).

Historical analyses of crime levels were largely dependent on police statistics and, given the nature of police–community relations and the police's priority on state security and the threat of paramilitary violence, there are sound reasons to be sceptical of these data.[51] Since 1988, a range of victimisation surveys were conducted that have added considerably to our knowledge of these issues. Northern Ireland participated in several sweeps of the International Crime Victims Survey (ICVS) (1989, 1996, 2000 and 2005). While there are inherent difficulties in making comparisons across a diverse range of countries, especially given the use of somewhat different methodologies (and in Northern Ireland's case, this changed over time), the ICVS nevertheless provides a very valuable source of information on victimisation rates in relation to some specific offence types.

The most immediately striking finding of the ICVS survey was that Northern Ireland recorded the second lowest victimisation rate – behind Japan – of the twenty countries included in the 1989 and 1992 surveys. The victimisation rate in Northern Ireland was in the range of 12.5–14.9 per cent (meaning that just over one in eight respondents had been the victim of any of the crimes covered in the survey in the past year), while the average victimisation rate across the other countries was in the range of 20.0–22.4 per cent.[52] In the 1996 ICVS survey, Northern Ireland was found to have the lowest victimisation rates of the eleven participating countries, a rate of 16.8 per cent, compared to the average of 24 per cent. The survey also found that respondents in Northern Ireland were the least likely to report offences to the police, and 'generally were more likely than those in most other countries to be unhappy about lack of interest from the police, the fact that they had not caught an offender, did not recover any property, and gave insufficient information'.[53] As Mayhew and van Dijk noted:

Crime in Northern Ireland has been very stable since 1988 according to both the ICVS and police figures. Risks are relatively low, even taking account of its low level of urbanisation. The fact that income dissatisfaction among young men is higher than elsewhere, and levels of night time social activity high – which on balance should increase exposure to crime – makes the Northern Ireland position even more notable. Clearly special factors act as a brake on crime.[54]

In a similar vein, the first Northern Ireland Crime Victimisation Survey conducted in 1994/5 found that levels of fear of crime, and perceptions of the likelihood of being a victim of crime, were considerably lower than in England and Wales.[55] Certainly, much official commentary on Northern Ireland highlighted its designation as a low-crime society. Within this narrative, low crime levels were repeatedly used to highlight its unexpected tranquillity and to juxtapose this with the violence of paramilitary groups. Thus, one Northern Ireland Office publication described Northern Ireland as 'the most law-abiding part of the United Kingdom',[56] while in a similar vein the Police Authority noted that: 'Community strife is limited to relatively small areas of Northern Ireland. In the main it is a beautiful country in which many people born elsewhere choose to make their homes and set up business.'[57] The difficulty with the 'surprisingly low levels of crime despite the Troubles'[58] thesis is that by homogenising Northern Ireland into the category of a 'low-crime society', it overlooks the enormous disparities in victimisation levels that exist across different communities and areas. It also overlooks the existence of what was in effect a small-scale war and minimises the scale and social impact of many issues which do not fall neatly within the parameters of crime statistics, for instance, the symbolic significance of a church or Orange Hall being burnt down, as opposed to other forms of vandalism.[59] Thus, Northern Ireland appeared to be something of a paradox: a low-crime society in terms of overall crime levels, while simultaneously having, at certain times, very high levels of specific forms of crime (typically related to the conflict) such as homicide and armed robbery. The conflict may have served to suppress particular forms of minor and/or property-based crime that victimisation surveys routinely measure, but for obvious reasons the more serious forms of crime,

Percentage that viewed the following as a 'big problem' in their area	Catholic Lower Working Class Urban	Protestant Lower Working Class Urban	Mixed Middle Class Urban	Catholic Small Towns	Protestant Small Towns
Drug Abuse and Dealing	24.4	11.9	0.5	23	7.5
Arson	8.5	6.4	1.3	0	0
Vehicle Theft	30.5	10.7	12.6	1.9	0.7
Joyriding	37.7	4.2	1.5	0.6	0
Punishment Beatings	17	1.7	0.1	0	0
Sectarian Harassment	4.7	2.8	1.9	0	0.7
Paramilitary Harassment	5.4	2.7	0	0.3	0
Police Harassment	10.1	2.2	0.4	0.3	0
Victimisation rate for any type of crime in last 12 months	24.2	21.7	25	20.4	14.5

Table 2.3: Crime, Harassment and Victimisation in Different Communities

Source: Adapted from David O'Mahony, Ray Geary, Kieran McEvoy and John Morison, *Crime, Community and Locale: The Northern Ireland Communities Crime Survey* (Aldershot: Ashgate, 2000), Tables 2.5, 2.6 and 3.1.

typically conflict-related, dominated public and political debate.

The Northern Ireland Communities Crime Survey was one attempt to highlight regional/community variations in victimisation, by surveying residents in communities across a range of different socio-political profiles.[60] As Table 2.3 demonstrates, the ranking of 'big problems' relating to crime and harassment shows considerable variation across the different communities, and the reported victimisation rates were considerably higher than that found in the 1996 ICVS survey.

The relationship between social class and crime victimisation is complex and uneven, although much research indicates that marginalised groups tend to experience higher victimisation levels across at least some forms of crime.[61] Table 2.3 indicates there is a notable variation in victimisation rates across the different communities, with 'Protestant Small Towns' having the lowest and 'Mixed Middle Class Urban' having marginally the highest. It is unclear why 'Mixed Middle Class Urban' communities had the highest victimisation rate, although it may involve a combination of their 'suitability' as 'targets' (by virtue of car ownership rates, home possessions, etc.) and consumption patterns, and higher levels of trust in the police and a greater willingness to report crime.

One striking feature in Table 2.3 is the variation in the extent to which these issues are considered 'big problems' in the different research sites. Each issue, and mostly by a considerable margin, was more likely to be viewed as a 'big problem' in 'Catholic Lower Working Class Urban' areas than in other areas, with 'Protestant Lower Working Class Urban' communities the next most likely to view them as such (with the exception of 'vehicle theft'). These findings are consistent with other research which highlights the overlap between material deprivation and exposure to crime and violence, and the starkly uneven impact that the conflict had on different communities.[62] Some of this variation can only be understood by considering the impact that the conflict exerted across the field of crime and the criminal justice system, and it is to those issues that we now turn.

The conflict, crime and policing

The conflict influenced the nature of policing and the wider field of crime prevention in several fundamental respects, and hindered the provision of an effective response to problems of crime and disorder.[63] First, it meant that security concerns dominated the policing agenda. Some areas of Northern Ireland were left largely untouched by the day-to-day violence, and policing in those locales reflected this relative tranquillity.[64] In other areas, particularly those in which the conflict was concentrated, policing became increasingly militarised and the great majority of policing resources were absorbed by the conflict. Although police primacy had been based on the intertwined goals of increasing the RUC's effectiveness while simultaneously increasing its legitimacy, it proved more successful in relation to the former than the latter.

After significant criticism of policing in the early years of the conflict, the RUC embarked on a major professionalisation strategy during the 1970s, but its enhanced role meant that it became increasingly embroiled in controversial policies and practices that undermined its efforts to secure widespread public support. Day-to-day security measures, such as roadblocks and stop-and-searches, were widespread and the weight of them fell disproportionately on Catholics. In the period 1972–6, some 251,008 house searches were carried out in Northern Ireland, when the 1971 census recorded only 427,434 households across the region.[65] These searches were concentrated in particular areas, with some homes searched repeatedly, producing stark disparities in experience across communities. For example, research with teenagers and young children found glaring differences in their first- and second-hand experiences of security measures. In one study, of the sixty Catholic youths interviewed, twenty-two had had their homes searched and nearly all the Catholic interviewees knew of friends' or relatives' homes being searched. House searching was 'virtually unheard of' among the Protestant interviewees.[66] McVeigh also reported major disparities in Catholics' and Protestants' experiences. He found that 51 per cent of 18–19-year-old Catholics claimed they had been harassed by the security forces, compared to 16 per cent of Protestant youths.[67] As Table 2.4 indicates, this perception that Catholics inevitably were the target for such policies had a damaging impact on their confidence in the police and in their support for various security measures.

In his authoritative overview of research on Northern Ireland, Whyte found the disparity between Catholics' and Protestants' levels of approval for the use of plastic bullets to be the 'sharpest division ... on any question in any opinion poll held in Northern Ireland'.[68] The asymmetry between their views on policing and security issues led him to conclude that 'there is an even greater degree of disagreement between Protestants and Catholics on security policy than there is on constitutional questions. Security issues remain an unhealed sore'.[69]

Second, and related to the above, the physical dangers arising from the conflict placed severe constraints on the

	Catholics Agreeing (%)	Protestants Agreeing (%)
Police treat Protestants better	55	12
Police treat Catholics better	0	4
Police try hard to stop Protestant attacks	46	86
Police try hard to stop Catholic attacks	82	74
House searches are used too little	3	26
House searches are used too much	35	3
Random searches of pedestrians are used too little	6	32
Random searches of pedestrians are used too much	41	3
Vehicle checkpoints are used too little	9	34
Vehicle checkpoints are used too much	40	8
Approve of 'shoot-to-kill' actions against terrorist suspects	7	61
Approve of increased use of undercover surveillance operations	25	90
Approve of use of plastic bullets during riot situations	9	86

Table 2.4: Public Attitudes to Policing and Security Measures

Source: Adapted from Ronald Weitzer, *Policing Under Fire: Ethnic conflict and police–community relations in Northern Ireland* (Albany: SUNY, 1995), pp. 86 and 137, using data from 1985 and 1990 surveys.

RUC's ability to respond to ordinary crime. The risks officers faced were sobering in scale. Between 1969 and 1998, 302 officers were killed as part of the conflict, and many more suffered life-changing injuries. In addition to these casualties, eighteen ex-RUC officers were killed in Troubles-related incidents, while approximately seventy officers committed suicide during the conflict, many of these surely related to emotional trauma arising from the conflict.[70] One Interpol study in 1983 found that Northern Ireland was the most dangerous place in the world to be a police officer, with a risk factor twice as high as the next most dangerous location at the time, El Salvador.[71] Practically all policing activities operated under this security threat, and 'routine' policing activities such as community police officers walking a beat required a level of protection that rendered them entirely symbolic and rather surreal affairs:

> two neighbourhood men walking their beat are accom-
> panied by at least sixteen soldiers, sometimes also by
> another squad of soldiers providing cover for those
> who are protecting the police, by two or more Land
> Rovers from the British Army and the RUC, and an
> Army helicopter.[72]

Third, many commentators alleged that the police had 'largely abdicated normal policing in troubled areas', allowing a 'policing vacuum' to develop there.[73] Typically, the police were criticised for not taking 'ordinary crime' seriously, and for enormous delays – hours and days – in responding to calls for assistance, if indeed they ever came at all. Security concerns were often the stated reason for this, but it generated enormous resentment and inevitably damaged the RUC's claims to be providing a service to all sections of the public. Some nationalist women who were victims of domestic violence 'reported that the police would not, or did not, come out to their homes', describing the RUC's response in the following terms: 'We are not going out there because it could be a set-up, anybody could phone us up and tell us that.'[74] One Catholic priest described an incident in Armagh that highlighted the concrete difficulties surrounding the RUC's response to calls from the public:

> I remember a young man being knocked down in Armagh in the street and he was killed. The man who killed him was a young UDR soldier, but he was in civvies. That was in a Catholic nationalist area. Obviously the police had to be called, but they wouldn't come. Often they wouldn't come without great reinforcements because of danger. But it was pouring with rain, and the body was lying on the street, and you weren't allowed to lift the body. I got the young man [UDR soldier] away, I took him to a police station in case something happened him; he was afraid himself. So the body laid there for a few hours and it was a terrible agony for the relatives. Finally, we said we have to take this body in. So, they [the RUC] never appeared at all. It was the same when you had break-ins or burglaries. They weren't coming for this, that or the other reason.[75]

While such delays inevitably were controversial, the reality is that RUC officers' safety concerns were well founded, and paramilitary groups repeatedly used reports of crime as a tactic to lure the police to ambush sites. One of the most infamous controversies of the Troubles – allegations of a shoot-to-kill policy against paramilitary suspects[76] – emerged from an incident in which three police officers were killed by a massive bomb. The IRA had stolen a tractor battery and, when the farmer reported the theft, the officers were killed on their way to investigate the report.[77] As one RUC inspector noted, security concerns permeated all aspects of how the police responded to reports of crime:

> People complain because we take so long to get to calls, but that's usually been because two weeks earlier the IRA called us up with the same story and were waiting there to kill us. There was a case where the home-help of an 88-year-old woman on Grosvenor Road rang us because the woman didn't answer her door. The IRA had taken the woman out so that the home-help would call us. And every case has to be treated like that. We checked up on the old woman. We checked up on the home-help, and she was who she claimed to be. We go around there, and there was a bomb by the back door. It didn't go off, though, luckily. Now, not every call is like that, but some are, and you don't know which ones are, so for every call you have to go through all these procedures.[78]

Fourth, the gathering of information and the cultivation of informants also impacted on police responses to ordinary crime. While this is an inherent aspect of policing world-wide, it assumes far greater importance in 'low intensity operations' such as that which prevailed in Northern Ire-land.[79] As one senior British Army officer noted, 'The key to smashing a terrorist organisation is the development of inside informers and the infiltration of their ranks.'[80] Following the police interrogation scandal of the late 1970s,[81] the RUC began to cultivate 'supergrasses' – paramilitaries-turned-informants – and between 1981 and '83 almost 600 suspects were arrested as part of some twenty-seven supergrass cases.[82] Controversies over the reliability of convictions based on their uncorrob-orated evidence gradually led to the demise of this par-ticular strategy. Within paramilitary organisations, in-formers were viewed as grave liabilities and were treated ruthlessly. Sutton estimates that eighty-two individuals were killed by paramilitary organisations – sixty-six by republicans and sixteen by loyalists – over the course of the conflict on the basis that they were informants for the security forces.[83]

Cumulatively, the police response to ordinary crime was substantially shaped by the need to generate and maintain a system of informants run by Special Branch, or by other covert units within the security forces. While such activities are inherently difficult to measure, infor-mants remained a highly contentious issue throughout the conflict and into the peace process.[84] Although typ-ically a 'hidden' part of the conflict, the scale of such activity and its implications for wider policing and security policy should not be underestimated. For example, one individual, Freddie Scappaticci, was a senior member of the IRA's internal security unit with responsibility for rooting out informants within the organisation. However, he was also an informer himself, working for the Force Research Unit, a covert British Army unit to the fore of counter-insurgency operations there. Described by a senior army officer as 'our most valuable spy' in the IRA,[85] it was alleged that he was involved in dozens of murders, and that the Force Research Unit may have participated in the murders of others to help protect his identity. On foot of the scandal, a senior British police officer was appointed with a team of forty-eight detectives to investigate the allegations.[86] Scappaticci died in 2023, and the investigation into his activities continues.[87] In another prominent example, Denis Donaldson, who had been in the IRA and was a prominent member of Sinn Féin, working closely with its leaders Gerry Adams and Martin McGuinness, was uncovered as an agent of the security forces.[88] Such cases highlight the extent to which paramilitary organisations were infiltrated by the security forces and how the British government was in a position to influence the course of the conflict from within these groups.[89]

The reality was that the security forces needed information to counter paramilitary activity, and those suspected of criminal involvement – whether related to the conflict or not – were a crucial means of obtaining such information. This inevitably generated conflict within the RUC, as officers involved in various aspects of crime investigation and detection found that security considerations impinged on or hampered their activities in various ways. One superintendent in the RUC Drugs Squad described the impact that Special Branch had on conducting police operations against criminal suspects:

The conflict made drug enforcement very difficult. To actually search a house in West Belfast was a major operation during the Troubles. You had to have maybe 20 uniformed police, the same number of soldiers. That took hours to organise. You had to get specific clearances from various groupings – Special Branch – within the force, because you had to make certain you weren't impacting on an operation that they were doing. And inevitably by the time you got there the information was dated by a number of hours or a day. Same with surveillance. During the Troubles, all surveillance was controlled by central groupings within the RUC. Again, it was controlled very much by the need to counter terrorism, terrorism was given the highest priority. So if we were doing a surveillance operation in Belfast and I got a call from Special Branch saying 'Could I stop the operation?' I had to do it, because a terrorist operation was developing from another part of Belfast or something. So you had to get clearance to do that, and they could just pull the plug whenever it suited – didn't have to give me an explanation or anything. Very frustrating. And it's inevitable that some people who are drug dealers are also of use to groupings within any organisation who are interested in terrorism. So I had to get clearance to search houses and if there was a conflict of interest with informants, I inevitably lost out. It happened occasionally ... and when it does happen it does cause a problem because people within the drug squad work out that that person is working for another group, and it was a bit disappointing.[90]

It would be hard to overestimate the influence that Special Branch exerted over the field of policing and security. The Patten Report noted that it comprised 850 officers (some 10 per cent of the regular RUC at the time), with a support unit of 280 regular officers, and a training unit of a further 90 officers.[91] While many of its activities were shrouded in secrecy and will likely remain so, it is clear that its role in state security enabled it to operate with considerable freedom from oversight. It was also repeatedly implicated in scandals relating to collusion between the security forces and loyalist paramilitaries.

Collusion was a uniquely contentious issue for the seriousness of the concerns it raised in its own right – state involvement in or support for criminal activity, including murder – while also for the challenge it posed to official claims of impartiality, professionalism, accountability and protection of the lives of the state's own citizens.[92] Although some allegations surrounded collusion between the security forces and republicans (such as in relation to the killing of Billy Wright, a loyalist paramilitary), the overwhelming majority involved collusion with loyalist paramilitaries. Collusion took different forms, spanning a continuum from passive to active support. It included cases where: members of the police/army were also members of loyalist paramilitary organisations; information was passed between the security forces and paramilitaries, particularly in terms of helping to identify targets and plan operations; weaponry was provided to (or not prevented from reaching) paramilitary organisations; agents or others were permitted to commit serious crimes, including murder; murder targets were not warned or protected; information was shielded from the RUC's criminal investigation department; and investigations into collusion were derailed, including setting on fire the building in which the Stevens inquiry into collusion was based in a deliberate act of arson.[93] Instances of collusion continued into the years after the 1994 paramilitary ceasefires. For example, in a highly critical report into collusion between the police and loyalist paramilitaries, the Police Ombudsman noted the scale of some of the issues involved. She stated that 'some informants were able to continue to engage in terrorist activities including murders without the [Criminal Investigation Department] having the ability to deal with them for some of those offences'.[94] She concluded that a 'culture of subservience to Special Branch had developed within the RUC' such that it had 'acquired domination over the rest of the organization'.[95]

Much attention has focused on prominent cases such as the 1989 murder of solicitor Pat Finucane but, given the covert nature of collusion, it is unlikely that the full scale of its prevalence or impact will ever be known. The use of loyalist paramilitaries as a proxy for the security forces ensures that lines of direct involvement are muddied, and the knowledge that political leaders had of such events or any authorisation they gave for them is likely to remain unclear. However, one indication of collusion's impact is highlighted by the fact that a major arms shipment to loyalists was permitted into Northern Ireland in 1988 with the knowledge of the security forces. It may have been allowed through partly to protect an informant's identity, or there may have been a breakdown in the surveillance operation, but it dramatically increased loyalist paramilitaries' operational capacity. In the seven years prior to the arms shipment, loyalist paramilitaries killed eighty-two people. In the seven years following the shipment, they killed 224 people.[96] Collusion continues to be one of the major sources of controversy relating to the Troubles, with the emergence of new evidence, including that the security forces helped loyalist paramilitaries specifically target the families of suspected republican paramilitaries,[97] only adding to those concerns.

With the policing of ordinary crime severely hampered by these various factors, the 'policing vacuum' in Northern Ireland remained a major concern in communities with high levels of victimisation. With an ongoing demand for an effective response to crime and disorder, paramilitary organisations entered this distorted and volatile policing environment.

Paramilitary punishments and alternative justice

As with many other conflict settings, the difficulties surrounding the legitimacy and effectiveness of the state system of justice ensured that a system of 'alternative justice' developed in Northern Ireland, largely comprising a system of punishments administered by paramilitary organisations. It is important to note that while paramilitary organisations claimed to be fighting a war against (republicans) or in support of (loyalists) the state, their activities were not limited to this, and included substantial involvement in different forms of crime.[98] Thus, alongside paramilitary involvement in politically motivated crimes – murders of members of the security forces, bomb attacks, and so on – was involvement in a range of other crimes to secure organisational or personal advantage. Large-scale organisations need resources to run effectively, and this was as true of paramilitary organisations as it was of any other type. Throughout the Troubles, paramilitary organisations engaged in extortion, smuggling, counterfeiting and drug trafficking, among other things, to fund their activities. At times, and depending on the specific context, they worked in collaboration with criminal gangs, while at other times they were in deadly opposition to one another. Much paramilitary 'ordinary' crime was funding-related, but members of paramilitary organisations also used their position and reputation to engage in crime for personal reasons. Nevertheless, paramilitary activity also extended to committing crime for social purposes, including shooting and assaulting alleged criminals in order to provide a policing service of sorts within their communities and thereby secure a degree of legitimacy.

The nature and complexity of 'alternative justice' in Northern Ireland evolved in response to the wider environment. As the Troubles started, 'no-go' areas developed where the police and army were kept out of particular neighbourhoods by barricades or simply the threat of riot if they ventured in. Various local 'defence associations' were formed in such areas, and these also took on a quasi-policing role, providing for the establishment of 'People's Courts' in some cases. For example, in the context of wholesale rejection of police legitimacy in republican areas of Derry, Doherty relates how as a leader of the local defence association, his responsibilities included investigating crimes in the area.[99] Some of this involved minor issues, such as a dispute over a pet bird which was returned following the issuing of a note to the woman in question: 'Please release one budgerigar immediately'. Other cases were infinitely more harrowing, including one investigation into the rape of a child. In that instance, Doherty ordered the apprehension of the offender and convened a local court to try him: 'He was our problem to solve and we had to satisfy the community's demand for his punishment.' The perpetrator admitted his guilt and, when asked what punishment should be imposed, each member of the locally established jury indicated he should be executed. The victim's family instead called for his life to be spared. With no scope to imprison him, ultimately the rapist was told that should he molest a child again, he would be executed without warning: 'A life had been saved, but a rapist had gone unpunished.' Such cases highlighted the practical and moral difficulties of assuming responsibility for law and order while operating outside of the formal criminal justice system and without any detailed framework or institutional resources to draw on. At one point, Doherty even requested the Irish Army to provide a house in Donegal, across the border from Derry, which could be used as a prison. As Doherty noted, the 'parallel state' they had created was a 'fragile thing'. In the early years of the conflict in particular, these initiatives were often specifically local in nature, but they also could take on a more institutionalised form. For example, during the ceasefire of 1974–5, the IRA established a series of 'community tribunals' which would in effect offer an alternative justice system to that provided by the state.[100]

While this relatively formal structure was short-lived, a system of alternative justice administered by paramilitary organisations continued throughout the conflict and beyond.[101] Typically, this system was mobilised by a member of the public making a complaint to a political party or group affiliated with paramilitary organisations, or directly to paramilitary organisations. If an investigation determined that the alleged perpetrator was guilty, he/she was then subjected to a form of punishment that ranged from warnings and curfews, to public 'shaming' (such as being tarred and feathered, or being forced to wear a sign publicly that specified the reason for the punishment[102]), beatings, shootings, and expulsions from the locality or from Northern Ireland as a whole. The application of penalties reflected wider public reactions as well as pragmatic political considerations. In 1991, for instance, the IRA stated that in response to public criticism over its use of physical violence, it 'has dramatically reduced punishment shootings of persistent hard-core offenders and has instead concentrated on a policy of ordering them to leave the country for specified periods of time'.[103] Similarly, following the 1994 paramilitary ceasefires there was a dramatic (albeit temporary) reduction in the number of shootings, alongside an increase in assaults, apparently on the basis that assaults were less likely than shootings to call the validity of the ceasefires into question.

The rationale for these systems of paramilitary punishments generally related to criticisms of the state system of justice. They were commonly depicted as a response to the 'policing vacuum' that had developed throughout the conflict, although clear differences marked the systems operated by republican and loyalist groups.

In republican areas, the difficulties of availing of the RUC were considerable. Even if some residents did not reject the RUC over its legitimacy, stark concerns remained over its ability to provide a meaningful and effective response to local problems of crime and disorder. Lengthy response times and the threat of intimidation also undermined residents' efforts to secure an adequate policing service.[104] In that context, republican paramilitaries were plausibly able to claim that the system of 'alternative justice' they administered was equivalent to a form of policing in the first instance.

In loyalist communities, the dynamics of paramilitary punishments were shaped by a somewhat different set of concerns. First, throughout the conflict, tensions persisted over the quality of policing in loyalist areas, and over concerns that some petty criminals enjoyed immunity from the police in return for the provision of intelligence on paramilitary activity and other issues.[105] Relations between loyalists and the RUC were particularly strained following the 1985 Anglo-Irish Agreement. The RUC's role in confronting protesters opposed to the agreement caused outrage among loyalists, and conflict between loyalists and the police escalated dramatically. In 1986, there were more than 500 loyalist attacks on RUC officers' homes, resulting in 120 officers' families being forced to move.[106] Nevertheless, considerable though these tensions were, the difficulties in relations between the police and working-class loyalist communities were not as acute as those which prevailed in republican areas. While loyalist paramilitaries could portray themselves to some degree as providing a policing service through the punishments they administered, the scale of the policing vacuum in loyalist areas was insufficient for them to depict themselves convincingly as the sole legitimate provider of policing services in those areas.

Second, while the Provisional IRA dominated republican paramilitary activity and had a centralised hierarchical structure, loyalist paramilitary organisations were more diverse and autonomous. Because of this, the difficulties of ensuring internal control were more pronounced for loyalist paramilitaries, and punishments were frequently used as a means of resolving organisational disputes rather than functioning predominantly as an alternative policing system.[107] Overall, Bruce suggests key underlying differences between loyalist and republican paramilitary organisations:

> loyalist paramilitary organizations differ from the IRA in being less well organized and less well staffed; less selective and skilful in their operations; less well funded and less well armed; more vulnerable to the policing of the security forces; more vulnerable to the propaganda work of the government's agencies; less well able to develop an enduring political programme and community base for their activities; more vulnerable to racketeering; and hence less popular with the population they claim to defend.[108]

These differences, according to Bruce, are largely attributable to structural factors, namely the degree of alignment with the state: being a pro-state paramilitary group, or an insurgent one. While the differences between loyalist and republican paramilitary organisations on particular issues may be small, cumulatively their impact is notable. For loyalists wishing to defend Northern Ireland, there were a range of legitimate routes available to do so: police, army, or other avenues. As such, recruitment to loyalist paramilitary organisations was from a relatively smaller pool, raising questions about the calibre and motivation of recruits. This in turn made them more susceptible to involvement in predatory and criminal behaviour and more susceptible to infiltration by the security forces. These dynamics are not specific to Northern Ireland, and involvement with criminality is a recurring feature of pro-state paramilitary groups globally.[109]

Notwithstanding the differences outlined above, providing a response to crime was one of the ways in which paramilitary organisations could claim to be addressing the needs of their constituent communities. Against the backdrop of high levels of social deprivation as well as the broader political conflict, the activities of petty criminals (known as 'hoods') were often the focus for major concern in specific areas of Northern Ireland.[110] Many of these concerns coalesced around the issue of joyriding.[111] In terms of prevalence, it tended to be mostly associated with Belfast rather than other parts of Northern Ireland, and within Belfast it was concentrated in nationalist/republican areas of the city, and west Belfast in particular. As noted above, in the Northern Ireland Communities Crime Survey, joyriding was ranked as the biggest crime problem in Catholic lower working-class urban communities, where 58 per cent of respondents stated they had witnessed it in their area over the past three years, in comparison to 10 per cent of respondents in Protestant working-class urban communities and 6 per cent in mixed middle-class urban areas.[112]

Although joyriding dates from the early decades of the twentieth century,[113] in Northern Ireland the development of a joyriding culture originated in the 1970s in part at least from the practice of stealing cars for use in barricades to prevent the security forces entering particular areas, or for similar purposes. While joyriding may initially have aligned with the street activities of republicans, it subsequently developed a different trajectory, and came to be associated with a youth subculture of risk-taking and bravado. McCullough and Schmidt described joyriders as 'expert show-offs',[114] while the expressive nature of their involvement in crime led Hamill to characterise their behaviour as part of a 'signalling game, played in order to attain and maintain prestige and status'.[115] Moreover, it also featured elements of defiance and a rejection of the various authority structures that prevailed in Northern Ireland. Joyriding was a highly emotive issue and the subject of ongoing demands for action to be taken to address it, not least due to the dangers it posed to joyriders and bystanders alike. Between 1971 and 1999, at least twenty-nine joyriders were killed (whether in accidents or by members of the security forces), and between 1990 and 2002 a dozen bystanders were killed by joyriders.[116] Drug dealers evoked a similarly hostile response from local residents who viewed them as preying on vulnerable individuals and undermining entire communities;[117] paramilitary organisations also viewed individuals involved in crime as vulnerable to police activity, including potentially becoming police informants. Along with others suspec-ted of involvement in crime (such as burglary, assault and sexual offences), these groups of predominantly young men bore the brunt of the system of paramilitary punishments.[118]

The graphs below show the level of paramilitary punishments by loyalists and republicans since the RUC began recording shootings in 1973 (assaults have been recorded since 1988). These inevitably underestimate the overall level of punishments, including assaults that did not require hospitalisation; and they omit expulsions. Between 1973 and 1998, a total of 3,410 punishment shootings and assaults were recorded. Of these, republican paramilitaries were responsible for 57 per cent (1,939), while loyalists accounted for 43 per cent (1,471). From 1973 until the mid-1980s, republicans were responsible for most shootings, but from 1986 to 1998 loyalist paramilitaries conducted more punishment shootings than republicans on all but two occasions (1989 and 1998). This probably reflects a higher level of activity by loyalist paramilitaries generally, violent feuds between different paramilitary groupings, and greater loyalist criticism of the RUC (as discussed above).

The sheer brutality of these assaults – typically administered to young males from areas of high deprivation, and sometimes proving fatal – generated much criticism.[119] The RUC chief constable wrote that 'Nothing less than broken limbs and battered bodies satisfies the power lust of the paramilitary godfathers who control such activities'.[120] While paramilitary punishment certainly may have functioned as one means of exercising territorial control,[121] it is undeniable that public demand played a significant role in the dynamics of these issues. One loyalist politician explained how he was obliged to tell members of the public 'to desist from asking

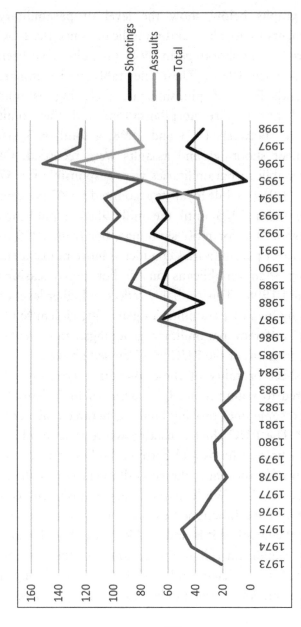

Figure 2.3: Loyalist Paramilitary Punishments, 1973–98

Source: PSNI

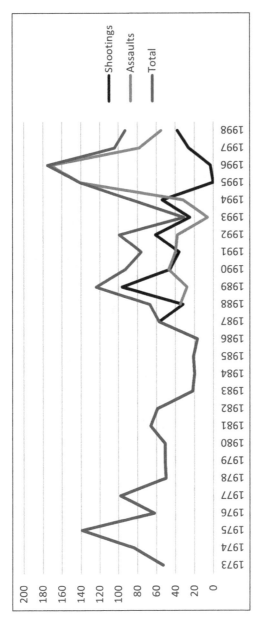

Figure 2.4: Republican Paramilitary Punishments, 1973–98

Source: PSNI

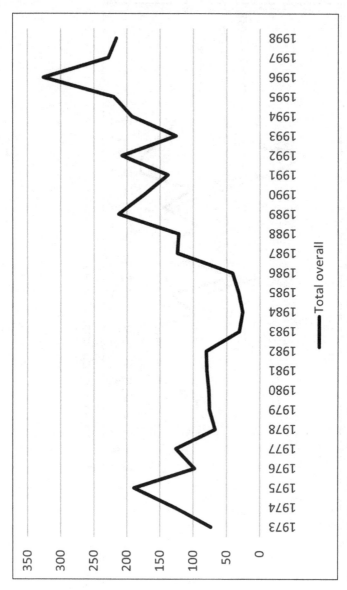

Figure 2.5: Total Paramilitary Punishments (Loyalist and Republican), 1973–98

Source: PSNI

paramilitaries, because that's what happens. They don't go trawling the streets, they don't go rapping on doors asking "Has anybody violated your property or person so that we can give them a good hiding?"' Similarly, an RUC sergeant acknowledged how some members of the public supported extreme punishments against 'hoods':

You hear all this talk about it being a terrible thing to do and it's just the provos keeping their hold on their community, but when you talk to people, you find that a lot of them want to see something done about crime. The thing is, see, lots of people say that the hoods are being shot in the wrong place. Instead of shooting them in the legs, they should be shooting them here [pointing to the side of his head].[122]

In the Northern Ireland Communities Crime Survey, O'Mahony et al. found that 36 per cent and 26 per cent, respectively, of Catholic and Protestant respondents in lower-working-class urban communities claimed to have reported crime to paramilitary organisations.[123] In a society wracked by conflict and high levels of deprivation, and with all the underlying difficulties surrounding policing, some level of public support for a paramilitary solution to crime problems is hardly surprising. In those extreme settings, it may mirror a wider public ambivalence towards paramilitary violence. In their analysis of the 1999–2000 European Values Survey, Hayes and McAllister found that a substantial minority of respondents expressed a 'lot' or a 'little' sympathy with the use of paramilitary violence.[124] In the case of Catholic respondents, 42 per cent claimed to have some sympathy for republican paramilitary violence, and 30.8 per cent claimed to have some sympathy for loyalist paramilitary violence. Among Protestant respondents, 24.1 per cent expressed sympathy for loyalist paramilitary violence, and 10.2 per cent expressed sympathy for republican paramilitary violence.

The concerns that these issues highlighted – the basis on which a political agreement might be forged, and the role that issues of crime and justice would play in this process – were much in evidence during the peace process that developed during the 1990s. It is to that period of uncertain peace and transition that we turn now.

Chapter 3

Transition: 1999–2022

A LTHOUGH THE PARAMILITARY CEASEFIRES in 1994 provided welcome relief from the violence of the conflict, the years immediately after were characterised by a complex blend of cautious optimism and wretched disappointment. While the level of violence diminished greatly following the 1998 Belfast Agreement, deep political divisions remained as evidenced by the need for further 'agreements' to address outstanding issues, and the social consequences of conflict were plainly visible. Sporadic violence, huge conflict over parades (most notably around Drumcree, in Portadown) and the flying of flags outside public buildings, protracted political negotiations, the IRA's decision to end its ceasefire (subsequently reinstated) by exploding a massive bomb in Canary Wharf in London, threats from 'dissident republicans' opposed to the peace process, and repeated suspensions of the Northern Ireland Assembly all ensured that any political progress seemed desperately fragile, if not illusory. There were more 'peace lines' – high walls erected at interface areas to provide a security barrier between loyalist and republican communities – after the conflict than there were during it. The Northern Ireland Executive's goal was to have them removed by 2023, but the Executive's suspension and some community support for retaining the peace lines ensures that they will likely remain in place for the foreseeable future.[1] Residential areas remain highly segregated, as is the education system: only about 8 per cent of school children attend integrated schools. Northern Ireland's suicide rate is the highest in the UK and rose significantly *following* the peace process,[2] and the prescription rate for anti-depressant medicines is the highest in the UK and one of the highest in the world.[3]

Yet these setbacks, uncertainties and crises masked significant changes to the underlying political dynamics: republican paramilitaries became increasingly committed to a political solution; the British government indicated its willingness to hold talks on the future of Northern Ireland; considerable international pressure was put on all the parties involved to pursue a peaceful settlement; and across Northern Irish society, there was a palpable sense that the conflict had entered its endgame, not least through the many commemorative events held for victims of the Troubles, indicating that the conflict was increasingly being viewed in the 'past tense'. After predictably fraught negotiations, in 1998 the political parties reached an agreement – the Belfast Agreement (often termed the Good Friday Agreement) – that outlined the basis of a political settlement. The impact of the agreement was uncertain, given that the Democratic Unionist Party (DUP) had walked out of the talks, and deep suspicion remained between the remaining parties, particularly mutual scepticism between Sinn Féin and unionist politicians. Further talks were necessary to resolve issues of power-sharing and paramilitary decommissioning, and although more people would die (the PSNI estimated that between 1999 and 2022, 115 individuals were killed in conflict-related violence within Northern Ireland – see Appendix), it seemed at last that the conflict was over.

The Belfast Agreement addressed many contentious issues, including the release of paramilitary prisoners. In respect of policing and the criminal justice system generally, the agreement specified that these issues would be addressed separately by independent commissions (respectively, the 1999 Independent Commission on Policing, and the 2000 Criminal Justice Review). Given the centrality of these issues to the peace process, delays and disagreements in resolving them contributed to further uncertainty and political instability. Nevertheless, a significant reform programme occurred across the criminal justice system. As Dickson noted, 'Today it is as if a new brush has been swept across the land. Virtually every aspect of the system has undergone root and branch reform, or is well on the way to that position.'[4] Clearly this was more evident in some sectors than others. The prison system, for example, did not receive the attention or resources directed towards policing, despite a number of pressing issues that required attention, including the treatment of women and young people, leading Scraton to describe this as 'a decade of stagnation'.[5] While the conflict may have shielded probation in Northern Ireland from some of the more dramatic policy shifts witnessed in Britain, since the 1990s there has been a shift away from a welfare ethos and towards 'public protection', mirroring developments in Britain, and there has also been a significant expansion of community supervision generally.[6] In relation to the court system, the routine use of Diplock courts was abandoned, although provision remains for jury-less trials in specific instances.[7]

While many aspects of these reform debates were controversial, the spectre of a new model of policing dominated much of the public debate on how the criminal justice system should adapt to a peaceful political environment. Given the pivotal role that policing and related aspects of criminal justice policy played throughout Northern Ireland's history, it is useful to consider those developments in detail.

Policing and the justice system

The Independent Commission on Policing (ICP), chaired by Chris Patten, was established to bring forward recommendations for future policing arrangements in Northern Ireland, and it published its report – *A New Beginning* (commonly referred to as the Patten Report) – in 1999. In its deliberations, the ICP noted the polarised nature of police–community relations, and the impact this had on the delivery of operational policing:

> In one political language they are the custodians of nationhood. In its rhetorical opposite they are the symbols of oppression. Policing therefore goes right to the heart of the sense of security and identity of both communities and, because of the differences between them, this seriously hampers the effectiveness of the police service in Northern Ireland.[8]

The ICP sought to outline a model of policing that drew on international best practice, and its recommendations fell into two broad spheres. First, it addressed the nature of the *police* institution, and sought to 'modernise' its organisational structures and practices and enhance its effectiveness. While some of these recommendations were banal (for instance, the recommendation that 'Police' should be written on police vehicles), others were more controversial, such as the proposed name change. Yet, as one ICP member noted, while the proposals relating to the police institution were 'very significant for Northern Ireland', in essence they were 'unexceptional – they apply principles that are routinely embraced elsewhere'.[9] The second strand of recommendations focused on *policing* more broadly. This included outlining the network of institutions that would assume responsibility for oversight and governance of policing, and while ensuring accountability was one core dimension of this, it also sought to 'deepen democracy' by focusing on the provision and governance of security generally – in effect, seeking to overcome the limits of state/market provision through greater community involvement, and partnerships across a range of actors and agencies. The main recommendations concerned measures to enhance accountability, governance and oversight; embed human rights within all aspects of policing; enhance the role of communities; increase Catholic representation within the police; and ensure that cultural practices and symbols were inclusive.

The response to the Patten Report was, to put it mildly, uneven, ranging from acclaim to outrage. While nationalists were soon calling for its full implementation, unionists were appalled at many of the proposed changes, particularly the 'loss' of the RUC's name. David Trimble, then UUP leader and the main unionist negotiator during the Belfast Agreement talks, described it as 'a gratuitous insult' to the RUC, and 'the most shoddy piece of work I have seen in my entire life'.[10] The DUP claimed that 'Patten's programme is that Protestants have to be ethnically cleansed',[11] and DUP leader Ian Paisley dismissed the report's recommendations as 'politically motivated; republican in character; calamitous to policing; prejudicial to the safety and security of law-abiding citizens; and the ultimate corruption of the integrity of the rule of law'.[12] The *Belfast News Letter* announced the report with a one-word headline, 'BETRAYED', while several 'Save the RUC'/'Defend the RUC' campaigns were launched, with a 400,000-signature petition delivered to the British prime minister. The Police Federation of Northern Ireland expressed its fear that the RUC was being 'airbrushed from history'. Across these protests, the sacrifice and bravery of RUC officers was repeatedly highlighted, and the proposed name change was seen as a provocative affront to their memory.[13]

The implementation of the ICP recommendations was tortuous and protracted, and it involved two separate acts of parliament (2000 and 2003) and a further two 'implementation plans' (2000 and 2001). Although the Police Service of Northern Ireland officially came into being in 2001, Sinn Féin only declared its full support for policing arrangements in 2007, at which point it began participating in the Policing Board and in District Policing Partnerships.

Notwithstanding this delay in implementation and the political battles surrounding it, the new policing arrangements received widespread praise as they bedded down. The Oversight Commissioner declared the reforms 'a great success',[14] while the chairperson of the Policing Board described the PSNI as 'a blueprint for democratic policing' and 'the most scrutinized and accountable police service probably anywhere in the world today'.[15] Chris Patten, the ICP chairman, called it 'the best working example of how to police a divided community',[16] and Clifford Shearing, also an ICP member, stated that:

> The PSNI has positioned itself internationally as an exemplary police organisation, largely because it has become a Patten-compliant organisation … there is widespread support for the view that the Patten Report, and its vision of policing, provides an example of the very best thinking about contemporary policing, and that it constitutes a benchmark that policing around the world can and should look to for guidance.[17]

Certainly, the Patten reforms brought about significant changes and clear improvements in the policing environment. This was particularly evident in a fundamentally reshaped institutional landscape of governance and oversight. The Policing Board and especially the Police Ombudsman quickly came to be viewed as robust entities. The Oversight Commissioner (which monitored the implementation process) was described by Patten as 'one of our best ideas',[18] suggesting that concerns over the extent to which their recommendations would be implemented loomed large in the ICP's discussions. The size and composition of the PSNI also changed considerably, as many officers left under a severance package, while under the 50:50 recruitment policy Catholic representation increased from 8 per cent in 1998 to 30 per cent in 2011 (at which point the policy was discontinued).[19]

Public satisfaction with the police continued to rise, gradually but steadily. Results from a series of Policing Board surveys conducted between 2007 and 2018 showed fairly high levels of overall satisfaction with the performance of the local police, with Protestant respondents marginally more positive than Catholics. Relatively high levels of satisfaction were also recorded in terms of the performance of the police across Northern Ireland as a whole, and assessments of police fairness. Across all dimensions, Protestant respondents reported higher levels of satisfaction with the police than Catholics did. For the latter two questions, however, the gap between Protestant and Catholic respondents was wider generally than for assessments of local police performance. This likely reflects higher levels of Catholic concern over the symbolism and practice of policing as an institution, compared to the more banal aspects of local (and relatively uncontested) policing.[20]

Although policing dominated much of the political and public debate during the transition period, it was clear that peace would also have major implications for the prison system, particularly in terms of reorienting itself from a model based primarily around the management

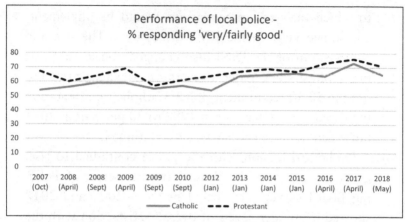

Figure 3.1: Public Assessments of Policing in Northern Ireland, 2007–18: Performance of Local Police

Source: Northern Ireland Policing Board Omnibus Surveys, 2007–2018 (Belfast: Northern Ireland Policing Board).

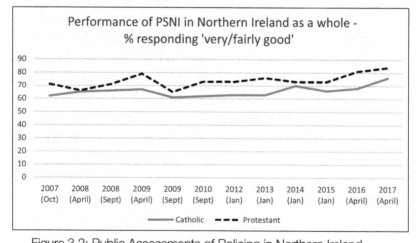

Figure 3.2: Public Assessments of Policing in Northern Ireland, 2007–18: Performance of PSNI in Northern Ireland as a Whole

Source: Northern Ireland Policing Board Omnibus Surveys, 2007–2018 (Belfast: Northern Ireland Policing Board).

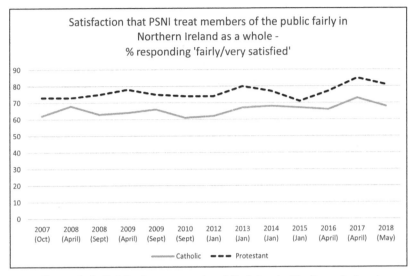

Figure 3.3: Public Assessments of Policing in Northern Ireland, 2007–18: Perceptions of Police Fairness
Source: Northern Ireland Policing Board Omnibus Surveys, 2007–2018 (Belfast: Northern Ireland Policing Board).

of paramilitary prisoners to one focused more on 'ordinary' prisoners. The conflict had left the prison system characterised by low staff morale, high costs, a prison estate shaped largely by security concerns, and little emphasis on issues of sentence management or prisoner welfare and reintegration.[21] One prominent consequence of the peace process was the release of paramilitary prisoners who met the qualifying conditions specified under the terms of the Belfast Agreement (including that the paramilitary organisation they were affiliated with was committed to and maintaining a complete cease-fire). Although this was a predictably controversial and emotive process, particularly for victims and their families,[22]

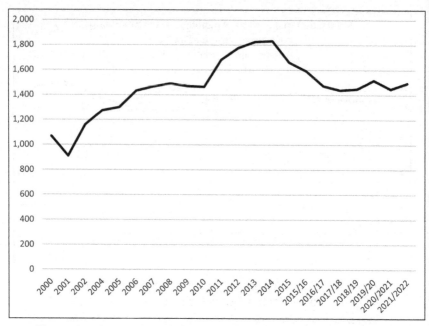

Figure 3.4: Prison Population of Northern Ireland, 2000–2021/2
Source: Nicola Carr, 'The Criminal Justice System in Northern Ireland', in
Steve Case, Phil Johnson, David Manlow, Roger Smith and Kate Williams
(eds), *Criminology* (Oxford: Oxford University Press, 2017); and Department of
Justice, *The Northern Ireland Prison Population, 2021/22* (Belfast: Stationery
Office, 2022).

in practical terms it was very successful. By 2013, a
total of 482 prisoners were released under the terms of
the agreement; of these, twenty-one were recalled for
having breached their licence, and in approximately half
of those cases this was for alleged paramilitary activity.[23]
By any measure, this recidivism rate was just a fraction of
that typically found in Northern Ireland and in most other penal systems.[24] The prison population dropped to 910
in 2001 (an imprisonment rate of fifty-four per 100,000
population), then doubled over the next dozen years,

before falling to 1,494 in 2021/2 (see Figure 3.4 below), at which point approximately forty individuals were serving sentences for paramilitary activity.[25] The rate of imprisonment in 2021/2 was ninety per 100,000 population, compared to rates of eighty-two in Ireland, and 135 both in England and Wales and in Scotland.[26]

In a further major change to the justice system, in 2010 the Department of Justice was established as part of new arrangements for the devolution of policing and justice, which had long been a sticking point in relations between the political parties. The devolution of policing and justice was identified as a priority by various political parties, and the Patten Commission recommended that it take place as soon as possible, but unionists remained opposed to its implementation until Sinn Féin declared its support for policing arrangements.

The assumptions surrounding devolution were straightforward and optimistic: it would lead to better, faster and more accountable government – local knowledge and expertise would generate a better understanding of the issues and provide an enhanced ability to identify solutions and mobilise resources, all under a more transparent and accountable political umbrella. While much political debate in Britain took place over the newly established system of police and crime commissioners,[27] and political developments in Wales and Scotland over devolution and independence respectively, in Northern Ireland the appeal of devolution was complicated by the fact that it had operated under devolved government from the inception of the state until the imposition of direct rule from Westminster in 1972. During this period, policing and the administration of justice generally was subject to direct political control by the minister of home affairs. While the peace process offered a new opportunity for the devolution of policing and justice, it was clear that unionists/loyalists and nationalists/republicans each wanted it, but for different reasons. As evidence of 'normalisation' and stability, it was of huge symbolic significance, but the focus of debate was on when and how it would happen; little consideration was given to what it would mean in practice.

The devolution of policing and justice functions finally took place in April 2010, following on from the devolution of most social and economic policy matters to the Northern Ireland Assembly established under the 1998 Belfast Agreement. David Forde of the Alliance Party was elected the first minister of justice, with responsibility for resourcing and the legislative and policy framework of the criminal justice system. The ministry had direct responsibility for the Prison Service, the Courts and Tribunals Service, the Forensic Science Agency, and the Youth Justice Agency. With key themes of (1) Safer, shared communities, (2) Faster, fairer justice and (3) Reformed Prisons and Youth Justice System, devolution may have seemed a straightforward means of securing a better delivery of justice. However, from the British government's perspective, the peace process also provided scope for a substantial reduction in the subvention from the British Treasury (which was approximately £7 billion sterling in 2007). In 2010, in the aftermath of the 2008 global financial crisis, the British government committed itself to an austerity programme, resulting in major cutbacks in public spending, including significant cuts to the public sector in Northern Ireland. The PSNI was not subject to the same level of cutbacks as police forces in England and Wales, but it was required to make savings of £135 million by 2014/15,[28] and further budget cuts have put significant strains on different aspects of operational policing, including the ability to investigate historical cases.[29]

These factors helped ensure that devolution's impact was less than envisaged. McAlinden and Dwyer suggest that 'the devolution of policing and justice has made little if any significant difference to the shape and direction of criminal justice policy and practice in Northern Ireland'.[30] While this may partly reflect the recency of its creation, the key driver of developments in Northern Ireland is not devolution, but rather 'policy trends elsewhere' (notably through policy transfer from England and Wales) and 'the legacy of the conflict'.[31] The volatility of the political context also undermined the potential for devolution to deliver significant change. In 2017, Sinn Féin withdrew from the power-sharing executive, which duly collapsed. This arose over concerns relating to DUP leader and first minister Arlene Foster's role in a disastrous renewable heat incentive scheme that may ultimately cost the taxpayer half a billion pounds, but it was clear that a range of other disagreements had also contributed to the breakdown in the working relationship between Sinn Féin and the DUP. After being suspended for three years, the assembly reopened in 2020, again under a power-sharing executive led by the DUP and Sinn Féin (with the other main parties forgoing the ministerial seats they were entitled to and instead becoming the opposition within the Assembly).

Further political uncertainty arose from the British government's decision in 2017 to withdraw from the European Union following the results of the 2016 'Brexit' referendum. The UK voted in favour of withdrawing from the European Union by a majority of 52 to 48 per cent, although in Northern Ireland the result was 56 per cent in favour of *remaining*. In 2017, the government invoked Article 50 of the Treaty of the European Union with a view to leaving the European Union, and it formally did so on 31 January 2020. As the border between Northern Ireland and the Republic of Ireland now became a *de facto* EU border, the question of how to reconcile the UK's withdrawal from the EU, the obligations of the Belfast Agreement in terms of free movement and identity, and the EU's desire to protect the integrity of the internal market led to the introduction of the Northern Ireland 'Protocol'. Any border is simultaneously a constraint and an opportunity: a constraint on the free flow of people and goods (and the daily inconvenience this posed for border communities), and an opportunity to exploit the different regulatory regimes and socio-political conditions that may exist in the two jurisdictions. The more different the two sets of regulations, the more they encourage a variety of illicit activity, smuggling particularly. Smuggling has been an enduring feature of life on both sides of the border since partition, and while historically it leaned more towards local activity,[32] the nature of global trade ensured that the EU was particularly attentive to the risks that smuggling posed to the integrity of its single market. Moreover, the return to a 'hard border' on the island of Ireland was seen as a significant threat to peace and stability.

The Protocol would avoid any new border infrastructure between Northern Ireland and Ireland by ensuring that Northern Ireland adopted the EU's regulations on goods and introducing new checks on goods between Britain and Northern Ireland: in effect, it established a customs border between Northern Ireland and Britain in place of a land border between Northern Ireland and the Irish Republic. Within loyalism this generated outrage, as the new regulatory 'border' between Northern Ireland and Britain led to considerable disruption and delay in transporting goods between both jurisdictions. Despite the relative advantage the Protocol gave Northern Irish businesses by enabling them to trade with the EU as part of the single market, unionists viewed it as a symbolic and material weakening of Northern Ireland's position within the United Kingdom. Against that backdrop, serious riots occurred in loyalist areas in early 2021, and the DUP refused to participate in the power-sharing Executive until the Protocol was overhauled or replaced (effectively suspending the Executive again). Following further negotiations, in 2023 the Windsor Framework was agreed between the UK government and the EU, comprising a more simplified set of customs measures to minimise disruption to trade between Britain and Northern Ireland. The DUP stated that these measures did not go far enough to meet their demands and – at the time of writing – still refuses to re-enter the executive; as a result, the Assembly remains suspended. During the 2023 local authority elections, Sinn Féin won the largest number of seats, and since Brexit there have been numerous calls for a 'border poll' which would entail a referendum on Northern Ireland's future. Given wider political and demographic changes, the future of the devolved government in Northern Ireland is unclear. The overall implications of Brexit continue to unfold, but unless and until these are resolved, Brexit has scope to re-ignite major social and political divisions within Northern Ireland, and to damage relations between the UK, Ireland and the EU for the coming years.[33]

Crime, victimisation and political transition

One might argue that the above developments are testament to a new social and political reality in Northern Ireland, and the difficulties and tensions that have been outlined are simply the predictable concerns that might arise in any transitional process. Despite the understandable appeal of such an assessment, it overlooks an important aspect of divided societies. When a militarised conflict ends, this does not mean that violence or upheaval disappears from that society altogether; rather, conflict may continue in other spheres that nevertheless exert a huge influence on the dynamics of the society involved, and that carry a huge cost in terms of violence, injury and social suffering.[34] The concern that peace would itself generate new challenges for Northern Irish society was noted by the Patten Commission:

> Non-terrorist crime in Northern Ireland is at relatively low levels compared with the rest of the United Kingdom. Many people have expressed to us the fear that crime levels may increase in the future – a perverse sort of 'peace dividend' ... Terrorism is thought in some respects to have suppressed ordinary criminality, because it has involved some people who might otherwise have turned to crime, and because it has resulted in higher levels of security alert which deter the ordinary criminal. A more normal security environment might therefore lead to more 'normal' criminality. The growth of the drug problem in Northern Ireland – still small by the standards of Dublin or Edinburgh but growing fast – was mentioned to us time and again in our consultations of public opinion. There are also concerns that some terrorist groups, or members of groups, may turn from terrorism to drugs or other forms of organized criminal activity.[35]

The post-ceasefire period oscillated between optimism at the apparent ending of the conflict, and despair at the slow pace of political progress and the continuance of inter-communal conflict and sectarianism. Between 1996 and 2004, a total of 6,581 incidents of sectarian disorder in interface areas were recorded in north Belfast alone.[36] Furthermore, between 1994 and 2002, some 939 sectarian attacks on 'symbolic property' (including Orange halls, Gaelic Athletic Association clubs, churches/chapels and schools) were recorded; during the period 1994–2000, 78 per cent of attacks on places of worship involved 'a fire or petrol bomb incident'.[37]

Concern over crime was a prominent aspect of much public debate during the peace process, both in terms of growth in organised crime, and the crime that might arise from the social changes of the peace process itself.[38] The issue of drugs was repeatedly highlighted as a symbol of a changing social order and of the negative consequences of peace.[39] Levels of paramilitary violence tailed off dramatically, although some 'spoiler' activities by groups opposed to the peace process occurred as they sought to destabilise the political environment.[40] Moreover, while the larger paramilitary organisations largely eschewed violence for political purposes, violence for 'social' and 'economic' purposes continued, including paramilitary punishments and fundraising activities.[41]

The organisational capacity and ruthlessness of paramilitary organisations gave their criminal involvement particular significance. In the aftermath of the 1994 paramilitary ceasefires, a group termed 'Direct Action Against Drugs' – widely considered to be a front for republican paramilitaries – murdered nine people between 1995 and 2001 based on their alleged involvement in drug dealing.[42] In 2001, loyalists murdered investigative journalist Martin O'Hagan following his ongoing reporting into loyalist involvement in criminality. In 2004, a branch of the Northern Bank in Belfast was robbed, with over £26 million stolen in a well-organised operation.[43] The Provisional IRA denied involvement, but was widely considered to be responsible. In 2005, following an altercation in a Belfast bar, Robert McCartney was stabbed to death by members of the IRA. Although the murder appears to have arisen from an interpersonal dispute, the fact that forensic evidence was destroyed before the police were able to enter the bar, and that witnesses were unwilling to provide evidence, demonstrates the power that paramilitaries could wield and the immunity they could enjoy.[44]

The interaction between organised criminal groups and paramilitary organisations was also highlighted as particularly significant. In 2005, the Independent Monitoring Commission, which was established to report on paramilitary compliance with the ceasefires, reported that 'because of this paramilitary involvement organised crime is the biggest long-term threat to the rule of law in Northern Ireland'.[45] Although the level of involvement and the rationale behind it varied across groups, the Organised Crime Task Force stated that all paramilitary organisations in Northern Ireland 'are heavily involved in organised crime both as a means of raising finance for their organisations and for personal gain'.[46] This included cigarette smuggling, fuel laundering, counterfeiting, extortion and drug dealing.

Hate crime also became a prominent issue as the number of such reported attacks increased considerably, leading Northern Ireland to be described as the 'hate crime capital of Europe'.[47] The police began recording incidents of racially motivated hate crime in 1996 and homophobic crime in 2000. Hate crime is broadly covered under public order legislation from the 1980s, and the more recent Criminal Justice (Northern Ireland) Order 2004 which provided scope for an increased sentence to be given to someone convicted of a crime if it was 'aggravated by hostility' towards various specified social groups. However, there are numerous concerns about the criminal justice system's response to these issues. In the period March 2007 to October 2010, for instance, a judge imposed an enhanced sentence under the provisions of the 2004 order on only eleven occasions. The rate at which an enhanced sentence is applied seems to have increased since then: in 2015/16, it was applied in 89 of 248 cases in which 'hate' was an aggravating factor and a conviction was secured.[48]

As noted earlier, debates about levels of recorded crime and victimisation in Northern Ireland highlight the difficulties in reaching conclusive findings on these issues, particularly amidst the social and political flux of the peace process, and the practices and procedures which arose from the new landscape of criminal justice institutions. In April 1998, a new system of recording crime was introduced (the 'new counting rules') under which the level of recorded crime increased from 76,644 to 109,053 offences, an increase of 32,000 offences from one year to the next. This reflected the police recording a higher volume of mostly low-level offences that previously had not been included within crime statistics (including approximately 12,000 minor assaults, and 20,000 offences of theft, burglary or criminal damage). Other additional changes in recording practices were made in subsequent years (discussed further below). This also followed an increase of almost 17,000 offences from 1997/8 to 1998/9 (under the 'old' counting rules). In effect, over a two-year period, recorded crime increased by 82 per cent. Furthermore, from 2015 on, the agency Action Fraud took responsibility for fraud and cybercrime offences previously recorded by the PSNI. As a result, the PSNI's recent 'standard' crime figures now exclude offences that were previously included (see Figure 3.5 below). Despite these changes and wider concerns about the reliability of police recorded crime figures, some trends are apparent.

In terms of *crime data*, in 1998/9 a total of 104,647 offences (109,053 offences when fraud is included) were recorded by the police in Northern Ireland. Over the following four years this increased steadily, reaching an all-time high of 138,132 recorded offences in 2002/3, before declining to 106,492 in 2019/20. The impact of the lockdowns and restrictions imposed in response to the Covid-19 pandemic are evident in the crime level for 2020/1, with 94,231 offences being recorded, a drop of 11.5 per cent on the previous year and the lowest level of recorded crime since 1998.[49] In 2021/2, following the easing of Covid-19 restrictions, the crime level rose to 106,621 offences, an increase of 13.1 per cent over the

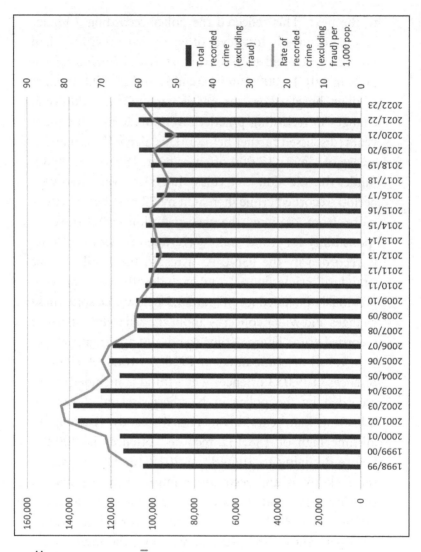

Figure 3.5: Recorded Crime in Northern Ireland, 1998/9–2022/3. Source: PSNI.

previous year; and in 2022/3, a total of 111,571 offences was recorded.

In terms of the *crime rate*, a similar pattern is evident. In 1998/9, sixty-two offences (excluding fraud) per 1,000 population were recorded, rising to eighty-one offences per 1,000 population in 2002/3, before subsequently falling to a rate of fifty-six offences per 1,000 population in 2019/20. By comparison, the crime rate for England and Wales in 2019/20 was significantly higher, at eighty-nine per 1,000 population. During the Covid-19 lockdowns in 2020/1, Northern Ireland's rate fell to fifty offences per 1,000 population, a drop of 38 per cent since 2002/3. Following the easing of Covid-related restrictions, the crime rate increased to fifty-six offences in 2021/2 and to fifty-nine in 2022/3.

The *detection rate* for offences (those 'cleared up' by the police, and more recently referred to in terms of the '*crime outcome rate*') in 1998/9 was 29.0 per cent, dropping to 20.1 per cent three years later. It rose to a high of 30.6 per cent in 2005/6, before again witnessing a substantial drop to 20.5 per cent in 2007/8, and subsequently rising to the mid-to-high twenties. In 2021/2 the detection rate stood at 28.6 per cent.[50] Although the initial drop in detection rates was frequently linked with the upheaval associated with the transformation of RUC to PSNI, and the departure of many experienced officers as a result of the new policies on recruitment and composition (given the scale of these issues, it would be strange if they had *no* effect), a PSNI analysis suggested that many of the changes in detection rates are due to changes in recording practices and evidential standards.[51]

Over this period, there was a significant change in the profile of recorded crime, through a substantial increase in the proportion of crimes against the person and a substantial decrease in property offences. Most of the crime reduction over this period arose from lower levels of crime in this latter category, particularly burglaries and vehicle offences. Looking at the breakdown of these figures by crime type, violence against the person and sexual offences increased from 19 per cent of recorded offences in 1998/9 to 49 per cent in 2022/3. Meanwhile, property-related offences (theft, burglary and criminal damage) dropped from 78 per cent of all offences in 1998/9 to 38 per cent in 2022/3.[52] Despite the overall reduction in recorded crime, the more detailed investigations required for violent offences posed a challenge for the police, perhaps partly due to reductions in police personnel and budgets, and the PSNI was criticised for failing to make adequate progress in its services to vulnerable victims.[53] Recorded crime levels also showed considerable variation across the region. While the overall crime rate in 2021/2 was fifty-six offences per 1,000 population, this ranged from a low of thirty-six in the 'Mid Ulster' and 'Fermanagh and Omagh' policing districts, to a high of ninety-five in 'Belfast City'.[54]

In essence, then, and regardless of the impact of new recording procedures, while crime levels in the immediate aftermath of the paramilitary ceasefires showed a slight decline, as the peace process developed there was a large increase in crime levels compared to during the conflict. This has since given way to a significant decline. Although crime levels have risen in the last two years (since the low associated with Covid-19 restrictions), the crime rate for 2022/3 is 27 per cent lower than the rate recorded in 2002/3.

If we turn to the International Crime Victims Survey sweeps, a somewhat different picture emerges. The 2000 ICVS found that while victimisation rates in Northern Ireland had risen since the previous surveys (1989 and 1996), these still remained comparatively low: again, the second lowest of the seventeen participating countries after Japan, and with about two-thirds the average victimisation rate.[55] However, in terms of the incidence and prevalence of criminal victimisation (respectively, the number of incidents per 100 inhabitants, and the percentage of the population victimised once or more in the previous year), the 2005 ICVS found that Northern Ireland's victimisation rate in raw terms showed a considerable increase on the previous studies, while its relative position within the ICVS rankings worsened.[56] ICVS data collection in Northern Ireland did change in the 2005 survey, although in a manner that enhanced its comparability with other countries.[57] At a time when crime rates across many parts of the world were decreasing, Northern Ireland's appeared to be increasing (see Table 3.1 below).[58] Note, though, that the last ICVS survey was in 2005, and if we look at other victimisation data (below) as well as police figures, the clear indication is that since the early 2000s, crime in Northern Ireland has declined significantly.

	One Year Prevalence Victimisation Rate		One Year Incidence Victimisation Rate	
	NI	Average for participating countries	NI	Average for participating countries
1989	12	17.2	18	28
1992	--	22.4	--	36.2
1996	11.8	20.3	18.9	32.4
2000	11.7	18.4	17.5	28.5
2005	20.4	15.7	35.2	24.4

Table 3.1: ICVS Victimisation Rates for Northern Ireland, 1989–2005

Source: Adapted from Jan van Dijk, John van Kesteren and Paul Smit, *Criminal Victimisation in International Perspective: Key Findings from the 2004–2005 ICVS and EU ICS* (The Hague, Ministry of Justice, 2007), pp. 237–40 and 249-52; appendix 9, tables 1 and 5. Note that the 'Average for participating countries' omits the UK, and so the figures here differ from those presented earlier.

Differences in methodology and timeframe means that caution is required in comparing across surveys, but the findings of the separate Northern Ireland Crime Victimisation Survey (which was first conducted in 1994/5, and since the early 2000s has been run annually) indicates that while victimisation levels did seem to peak around the turn of the century, there has been a steady downward trend since then.[59] The victimisation rate in 2019/20 was 6.9 per cent, a drop of over two-thirds from the 1998 rate of 23 per cent. The decrease in the rate of vehicle-related theft was quite remarkable, falling from 8.7 per cent in 1998 to 1 per cent in 2019/20, and this accounts

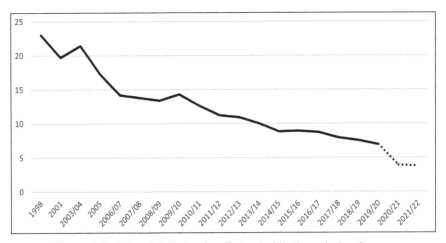

Figure 3.6: Crime Victimisation Rates in Northern Ireland, 1998–2021/2

Source: P. Campbell, A. Rice and K. Ross, *Experience of Crime: Findings from the 2019/20 Northern Ireland Safe Community Survey* (Belfast: Department of Justice, 2021); and K. Ross and M. Beggs, *Experience of Crime and Perceptions of Crime and Policing and Justice: Findings from the 2021/22 Northern Ireland Safe Community Telephone Survey* (Belfast: Department of Justice, 2023).

for much of the total decrease in victimisation rates over this period.[60] Overall, the risk of being a victim of crime in Northern Ireland is notably lower than in England and Wales (13.3 per cent in 2019/20), although this difference was more evident in relation to prevalence rates for household crime (5.4 versus 9.9 per cent) than for any violent crime (1.5 versus 1.9 per cent). The Covid-19 pandemic led to changes in the survey methodology, and the most recent rounds were conducted using telephone interviews rather than face-to-face interviews. The victimisation rate was 3.9 per cent in 2020/1 and 3.8 per cent in 2021/2.[61] Although these two surveys are not directly comparable to the earlier surveys, they nevertheless suggest that the broad trend of a significant reduction in victimisation levels over the last two decades remains the case.

In addition to changes in crime rates, beneath the rhetoric of the peace process the dynamics of crime continued to reflect underlying tensions across Northern Irish society. This was evident in relation to two issues in particular: the role of communities, and the legacy of the past.

Community and conflict

The peace process suggested that issues of state had finally been resolved in Northern Ireland, or at least decisively framed within the politics of consent. In that context, one might assume that communities would gradually come to play a greater role in crime prevention strategies. In Northern Ireland, however, while 'community' was often acclaimed within official discourse as epitomising decency, cohesion and resilience, it was also viewed with considerable scepticism and alarm; within this latter characterisation, communities were seen as inherently sectarian and politically immature, and in need of a neutral umpire (the British government, the Northern Ireland Office, the police) to keep them apart.[62] In the context of policing, it is noteworthy that despite the extended role for communities envisaged by the Patten Commission, the British government specifically rejected its recommendation that District Policing Partnerships (DPPs)[63] be given tax-raising powers to purchase additional services. The ICP placed great emphasis on DPPs as a means of realising its vision of 'policing with the community', and the tax-raising recommendation was a signal of the importance the ICP attached to them:

> We recommend that District Councils should have the power to contribute an amount initially up to the equivalent of a rate of 3p in the pound towards the improved policing of the district, which could enable the DPPB [District Policing Partnership Boards] to purchase additional services from the police or other statutory agencies, or from the private sector. They might choose to use the money for security cameras in commercial centres, or to fund youth club schemes: it would be for them to decide, in consultation with their local police.[64]

In making this recommendation, the ICP also noted that 'District Councils already have a general power to raise up to 5p in the pound for economic development'. This recommendation may have appeared innocuous compared to other more high-profile recommendations the ICP made, but it encroached on two core aspects of sovereignty – security and taxation – and it evoked a unionist nightmare in which republican paramilitaries might be transformed into a *de facto* policing provider.[65]

Running parallel to the Patten Commission's examination of policing, the Criminal Justice Review (2000) made recommendations for significant changes to the rest of the criminal justice system. It suggested that Community Safety Partnerships be established in each local authority area, and the government supported the provision of access to funding for these, a move that Patten Commission members thought was to ensure that DPPs 'withered on the vine'.[66] This appeared less the vision of empowered communities that underpinned the Patten Report, and more a continuation of centralised control over community involvement in the criminal justice system. The confusion between the organisations – DPPs, Community Safety Partnerships (CSPs) and the existing system of Community and Police Liaison Committees (CPLCs) – that occupied this increasingly crowded field of police–community consultation and community safety[67] led to a further review, and in 2012 a new system of Police and Community Safety Partnerships (PCSPs) was established to replace them. In 2014, Criminal Justice Inspection Northern Ireland (CJINI) noted positive initiatives in some PCSPs, but it found considerable variation across the sector in terms of activities and governance, as well as an absence of standardised ways of measuring their overall impact.[68]

These developments took place against a backdrop of wider changes in the political sphere (including devolution and a reduction in the number of local authority areas), but they reflected an ongoing concern over the nature and role of community involvement in the criminal justice system.[69] A wide range of non-governmental organisations in Northern Ireland provided services that fall under the umbrella of 'community safety',[70] but the greatest concerns related to paramilitary punishments. From 1998/9 until 2022/3, a total of 3,275 shootings

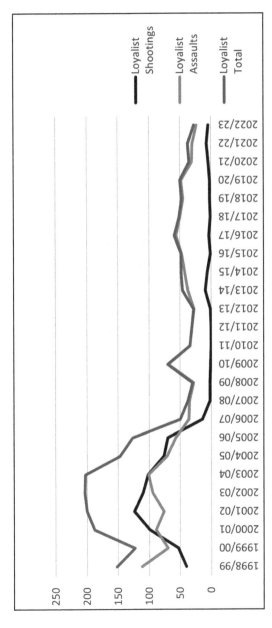

Transition: 1999–2022

Loyalist Shootings
Loyalist Assaults
Loyalist Total

250
200
150
100
50
0

2022/23
2021/22
2020/21
2019/20
2018/19
2017/18
2016/17
2015/16
2014/15
2013/14
2012/13
2011/12
2010/11
2009/10
2008/09
2007/08
2006/07
2005/06
2004/05
2003/04
2002/03
2001/02
2000/01
1999/00
1998/99

Figure 3.7: Loyalist Paramilitary Punishments, 1998/9–2022/3

Source: PSNI

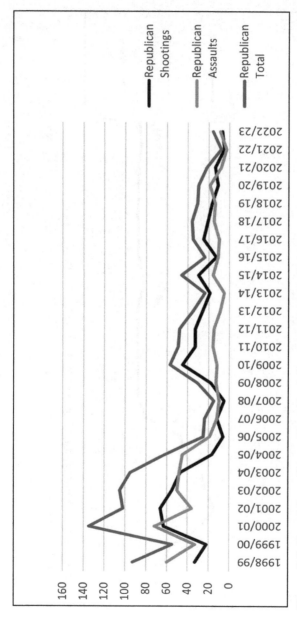

Figure 3.8: Republican Paramilitary Punishments, 1998/9–2022/3

Source: PSNI

Transition: 1999–2022

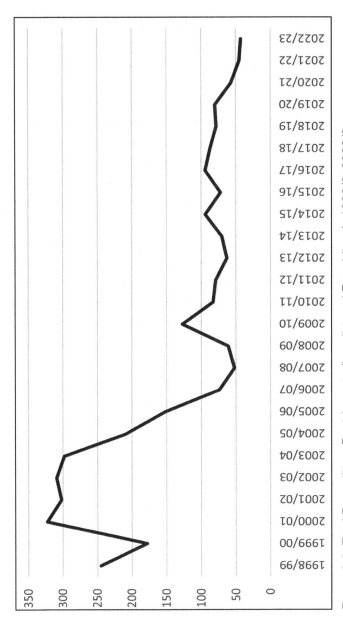

Figure 3.9: Total Paramilitary Punishments (Loyalist and Republican), 1998/9–2022/3

Source: PSNI

143

and assaults was recorded, 2,072 (63 per cent) by loyalist groups and 1,203 (37 per cent) by republican groups. The combined number of shootings and assaults over this period peaked in 2002/3 at 309, but since then it has declined, with forty-three being recorded in 2022/3.

During the 1990s, republican paramilitary groups began to move away from paramilitary punishments and develop a non-violent system of justice, based on a model of 'restorative justice'. The first scheme was established in 1998; it operated separately from the state and did not cooperate with the police. Under the umbrella of 'Community Restorative Justice Ireland' (CRJI) in republican areas and 'Northern Ireland Alternatives' in loyalist areas, gradually more schemes were developed. Following Sinn Féin's endorsement of policing arrangements in 2007, CRJI began cooperating with the PSNI. They were positively inspected by the Criminal Justice Inspector, and they continue to provide a range of services.[71]

Community support for the criminal justice system also relates to wider concerns over police effectiveness. While the new policing landscape was lauded as a success, much of this was due to the establishment of robust new institutions of police governance and oversight. The reality was that in terms of operational policing, the Patten Commission's vision of 'policing with the community' remained largely aspirational, and it was clear that hostility between police and public persisted in many communities, reflected in Sinn Féin's long delay in endorsing policing arrangements. Some examples of these difficulties are worth noting. In one instance, the commander of Rosemount PSNI station in Derry noted that only '12 people had visited the station between October 2003 and October 2004'.[72] In another example, police officers apparently refused to enter the Short Strand area in Belfast in pursuit of three teenage males who had assaulted a girl, due to concerns that the officers would be attacked.[73] Even by 2006, only 35 per cent of the PSNI's District Command Units 'claimed to be carrying out operational policing under "normal" conditions'[74]. The Oversight Commissioner highlighted the disjuncture between public expectations and the operational limitations of 'normal' policing:

> Successful policing must be about effective results and outcomes that meet the expectations of the communities and residents of Northern Ireland. That goal has not yet been reached ... The reality of capacity issues such as resource restraints, call and response management, crime and clearance rates, coupled with the time it takes to build trust relationships, all point to an 'expectation gap'. Normalised policing is quite simply a complex, difficult and expensive business that can never fully satisfy client demand.[75]

As ever, aggregate-level data hide the complexities involved in unravelling people's concerns over crime and disorder, as well as responses to those, and concerns over policing were experienced differentially across specific locales. In one study conducted in the New Lodge, a republican area in north Belfast, it was clear that in

the immediate aftermath of the ceasefires and with uncertainty over political progress and stability, many
residents felt problems of crime and disorder were being addressed neither by the police nor by paramilitary
groups. These issues were complicated by high levels
of victimisation – between six and twelve times higher
for vandalism, burglary and physical assault than the
victimisation rates reported by the Northern Ireland
Crime Victimisation Survey – and low levels of reporting these crimes to the police.[76] Even with the new institutions of police oversight well established, local perceptions of whether policing had improved or not were
strongly associated with instrumentalist assessments of
police performance, and in this marginalised area, with
no real experience of the limitations of 'normal policing',
residents were deeply critical of police responsiveness
and effectiveness.[77]

The legacy of the past

While the Belfast Agreement and related negotiations appeared to move Northern Ireland on to a new phase of
its history, there was no leaving the past behind. International experience suggests that measures to deal with the
past are an important feature of processes of transitional
justice, whether for purposes of truth recovery or political reconciliation,[78] although clearly it does not apply
equally to every society.[79]

In Northern Ireland, the scale, intensity and duration
of the conflict left a harrowing legacy, and unresolved

issues from the conflict and competing narratives of victimhood were prominent political issues.[80] Despite (or perhaps because of) the prominence of these issues, there was no widespread agreement on the need to address the past, still less on how it might be achieved. In its deliberations, the ICP noted the emotional intensity and cathartic quality of many of the submissions received and the contributions made at public meetings. In evidence to the US House of Representatives Committee on International Relations, Patten recalled one particularly raw episode:

> I can remember a meeting in a little village cinema in Kilkeel, a fishing village in the shadow of the Mournes. Protestant fishing fleet, Catholic farmers in the hinterland. We had a noisy and quite a good meeting. At the end of it, I made the sort of speech that we all can make terribly well as politicians about reconciliation and healing and hope. At the end of it, after I had finished, to my consternation I saw a little lady at the back of the cinema getting up to say something. I sat down rather nervously. She said, 'Well, Mr Patten, I have heard what you say about reconciliation and I voted yes in the referendum campaign, but I hope you will realise how much more difficult that is for us here than it is for you, coming from London. That man there murdered my son,' and it was true.[81]

Despite such widespread trauma, the ICP's mandate was to propose future policing arrangements rather than investigate previous policing controversies: 'We were not charged with a quasi-legal investigation of the past. If there is a case for such inquiries, it is up to government to appoint them, not for us to rewrite our terms of reference.'[82] One could argue that this was a missed opportunity, given the longstanding impact that scandals from the Troubles had on levels of public support for the police, collusion chief among them.[83] But equally it is clear that these issues extended far beyond policing and require a bespoke societal-level means of addressing them.

The British government established a Consultative Group on the Past to consider some of the issues involved in this process. While it recommended that a Legacy Commission should be established to deal with the past, its recommendation that a sum of £12,000 (in effect, a recognition payment) be given to the nearest relative of everyone killed in the conflict generated enormous controversy and exposed some key fault-lines in this debate, for appearing to equate all victims of the conflict, regardless of their role.[84] Chastened by this, the British government allowed these issues to drift. In another separate development, the PSNI established a Historical Enquiries Team (HET) to investigate the approximately 1,800 unsolved killings from the conflict.[85] This involved creating dedicated units to review the police investigations carried out at the time and any available evidence. While bringing charges against suspects was one potential outcome of this process, for the most part it simply yielded information that could be provided to victims' families and thereby give them some degree of closure.

Clearly, this model of investigation may provide answers to outstanding questions in individual cases, but it does not constitute a robust model for addressing such issues at a societal level. While the past continued to gnaw at efforts to maintain political progress, there is a further set of consequences to the absence of an agreed way of addressing the legacy of the conflict. As the Oversight Commissioner noted, the focus on policing the past is costly both financially and in terms of developing political agreement over shared priorities for the future.[86] These issues have also involved a range of criminal justice agencies in high-profile controversies. In a review by Her Majesty's Inspectorate of Constabulary, the HET was criticised for treating cases where state involvement was alleged 'less rigorously' than other cases.[87] The Police Ombudsman investigated several high-profile cases in which collusion was alleged, and reached damning conclusions.[88] However, this was accompanied by claims that the Northern Ireland Office sought to influence the investigations by downplaying any criticisms made of Special Branch in particular, and in the aftermath of this damaging controversy, Al Hutchinson retired from his post as Ombudsman in 2011.[89] These controversies and budget cutbacks saw the HET being disbanded in 2014. A new agency, the Historical Investigations Unit, was proposed to continue this work, but its establishment was delayed due to political disagreement on how best to address legacy issues overall. In the meantime, the PSNI's Legacy Investigations Branch continues to investigate historical cases.

The destabilising impact of unresolved legacy cases was also evident when, in 2014, Gerry Adams, the president of Sinn Féin, was arrested and questioned by the PSNI for four days over his alleged involvement in the 1972 abduction and murder of Jean McConville,[90] one of the 'disappeared' (those who were killed by paramilitary groups but whose bodies were never recovered). No charges were subsequently brought against Adams. On an ongoing basis, other legacy cases highlighted the difficulties of providing robust investigations into past events. For example, in 2020 the Public Prosecution Service (PPS) announced that it would not be prosecuting RUC officers allegedly involved in several killings (including the death of nine-year-old Patrick Rooney, the first child to be killed during the conflict in Belfast) on 15 August 1969 – fifty-one years after the events themselves. The PPS concluded that there was 'no reasonable prospect of conviction for any offence'.[91] In 2021, the PPS also indicated that it would not be proceeding with the prosecution of 'Soldier F', who was accused of murdering some of those killed on Bloody Sunday in 1972, again citing no reasonable likelihood of securing a conviction; after the family of one of the victims successfully appealed, in 2022 the PPS announced it would be resuming the prosecution.[92]

By any measure – whether political fallout or financial and organisational resources – the legacy of the past has had a major impact on the operations of the criminal justice system. The Criminal Justice Inspectorate of Northern Ireland noted that 'The criminal justice system alone is neither constructed to deal with the broad issue of the past, nor is it able to deliver the comprehensive answers society demands'.[93] It estimated that 'some 40% of the PSNI overall serious crime capability was being used in legacy matters' (in addition to HET resources).[94] In one of his last press conferences before stepping down as PSNI chief constable, Matt Baggott described the challenges of dealing with the past as 'debilitating and toxic to confidence', a statement that has only gained further credence in the years since then.[95]

In July 2021, the British government unilaterally announced plans to end prosecutions for all Troubles-related killings committed prior to the 1998 Belfast Agreement.[96] While this may have been intended to remove the threat of prosecution against members of the security forces in the first instance, it effectively amounted to an amnesty for all protagonists. Within Northern Ireland it generated strong criticism from across the political spectrum and from a range of human rights organisations.[97] Whether this specific proposal proceeds or not, the past continues to cast a long shadow over Northern Irish society and this is unlikely to change until concrete steps are taken to address legacy issues arising from the conflict.

Conclusion

THIS BOOK HAS charted the dynamics of crime and conflict in Northern Ireland over the course of a century, analysing these issues against the different backdrops of stability, protracted violence and transition. This concluding chapter summarises the main findings and considers the implications of Northern Ireland's experiences.

Crime and conflict in Northern Ireland

The extreme violence that accompanied the establishment of Northern Ireland was in stark contrast to the relative tranquillity and low levels of crime that prevailed through much of its early decades. The stability of the Stormont era was partly maintained by sheer political dominance and control over governmental institutions, and this dominance largely played out without recourse to overt violence. Alongside these political divisions, community structures were characterised by tradition, religiosity, family and locality and, of course, emigration. While some unknown level of victimisation (such as domestic violence or abuse in institutional contexts) went unrecorded, political divisions and community structures alike helped give rise to the low levels of crime that characterised Northern Ireland through these decades.

As the Troubles erupted, the scale of violence increased exponentially. While its devastating effects continue to echo, the dynamics of the conflict may have inhibited the growth of crime in several ways. The extensive security system and the regime of paramilitary punishments

ensured that Northern Ireland was heavily 'policed'. Even if this was skewed towards security issues, it inevitably affected levels of recorded crime in various ways, whether through deterrence or a reduced willingness to report crime to the police. In addition, the segregation that the conflict deepened also enhanced the impact of underlying community structures and resulted in a greater emphasis on informal social control mechanisms within local settings.[1] The scale of paramilitary punishments also demonstrates that many instances of crime were dealt with informally rather than through the formal criminal justice system.

Despite concerns over the reliability of official crime figures and victimisation data alike, this produced the 'paradoxical' outcome whereby Northern Ireland had a high level of some specific crimes (such as homicides related to the conflict) but a relatively low overall level of crime, albeit this was very unevenly distributed across Northern Irish society.[2] In some ways, this may be a predictable outcome given the nature of Northern Ireland: a society that was highly traditional, conservative, religious and segregated; and a political landscape founded on division, maintained through domination, and ultimately erupting in an extended violent conflict. Nevertheless, the juxtaposition between these two extremes remains striking. As Cairns observed:

These statistics therefore leave the reader a choice – either to rejoice that 'ordinary' crime in Northern Ireland is running at a fairly low level or to weep for its higher murder rate. Certainly if one accepts that the vast majority of the murders are at least politically inspired then one gets the picture of a fairly schizophrenic society where strict moral ethics are still the order of the day – except of course where politics are concerned. However one interprets these data they do make the point that the immorality or amorality of political violence in Northern Ireland has apparently not generalised to other areas of behaviour and thus in one sense 'war-torn Ulster' is actually a relatively crime-free and moral society.[3]

While some may choose different terminology from Cairns, the fact remains that the social upheaval of a widespread and sustained violent conflict did not usher in a new reality of Northern Ireland as a high-crime society. The organisational capacity of paramilitary groups (and of organised criminal gangs in the aftermath of the conflict) enabled them to perform acts of violence that exceeded what any individual would be capable of, but this was largely contained within specific parameters. Individual pathology or personal gain did not seem to be the primary motivating factors behind this violence. While these campaigns arose against a backdrop of political division, they were sustained by the participants' communal, organisational and micro-level solidarities: their sense of group affiliation and interpersonal loyalty.[4] The social consequences of this violence were devastating in so many ways, but it did not result in the increases in levels of ordinary crime forecast by many commentators. While overall crime levels did increase, many forms of crime remained at a relatively low level throughout the conflict, even as some 3,700 people lost their lives and many more thousands suffered terribly. The conflict facilitated particular forms of 'ordinary' crime, but its greater impact probably was to suppress crime through enhanced levels of policing and surveillance, and through the adaptive measures people took in response to the conflict. At a community level, this generated high levels of segregation and, with it, high levels of enforced cohesion. Cumulatively, these factors may have ensured that while levels of 'ordinary' crime increased, they did so moderately and due to underlying social changes rather than because of the disruption caused by the conflict.

One feature of the 'peace dividend' was, ironically, an initial increase in recorded crime levels. While this challenged Northern Ireland's historical characterisation as a low-crime society, it was not unexpected given the upheaval associated with the peace process, as well as the opportunity it generated for new criminal enterprises. Moreover, the violence of the conflict masked other social changes that had occurred in its shadows, including a general rise in crime in Northern Ireland (and most other countries) since the 1960s. The situation was further complicated by extensive restructuring to policing and the criminal justice system generally, as well as significant changes in crime-recording practices. Additionally, victimisation surveys which had previously depicted Northern Ireland as an outlier in comparison with other European or industrialised societies now found that its victimisation rates increased markedly while those of other societies were diminishing. More recently, however, and looked at in the round, the initial post-conflict increase in crime has been followed by a very large decline. In effect, this mirrors the reduction in crime experienced in many other western societies, albeit with a time lag. As with elsewhere, it seems likely that enhanced security measures – particularly in relation to car crime, burglary and theft – account for a significant proportion of this drop.[5]

Overall, comparatively low crime rates have been an enduring feature of Northern Irish society. The underlying political divisions might be thought to have destabilised society, but when these erupted into widespread violence and conflict, the impact on levels of 'ordinary' crime was relatively low. Crime did increase as the conflict wound down, and this is in line with international experience.[6] Yet the concerns that peace would produce a vacuum which would be filled by a toxic combination of new criminal alliances in pursuit of new criminal opportunities have not materialised to the degree some had forecast.[7] The crime–conflict nexus in Northern Ireland is partly shaped by the very dynamics of the conflict: context is crucial. Where some degree of legitimacy and community support is essential to the activities of paramilitary groups – this is particularly the case for insurgent groups rather than pro-state groups – there are strong incentives to avoid involvement in crime unrelated to their specific organisational goals.[8] If legitimacy is less crucial to the organisation's activities and effectiveness, then a different logic applies. In both situations, there is a trade-off between criminality and legitimacy. Over the course of Northern Ireland's history, the legitimacy needs of paramilitary groups was itself a crucial factor in shaping the nature, scale and dynamics of crime. This varies according to the nature of individual paramilitary groups and their relationship to the communities and interests they purportedly represent. However, to the extent that it did apply to particular groups, it functioned to enable paramilitary crime committed for organisational and social purposes, and to suppress rather than promote crime committed for personal gain.

If Northern Ireland's low crime rate is a familiar finding, it is one that should also be supplemented with the simple reality that when one scratches beneath the surface, the experience of crime was felt very unevenly across different regions and communities. Although Northern Ireland covers only a small geographical territory, vast differences in experiences of crime were evident across even short distances and community boundaries. Some groups were left largely untouched by crime and victimisation; others had their lives profoundly impaired by it, where it layered one additional burden on top of economic disadvantage and political violence.

As other commentators have noted, one of the key tasks of criminological research on Northern Ireland is to disentangle the assumed coherence of the imagined communities of unionism/loyalism and nationalism/republicanism and tease out the impact and implications of these 'divisions and differences'.[9] Important issues here include addressing the vulnerabilities of different social groups whose experience might have been obscured or ignored during the conflict, including victims of domestic/intimate violence and hate crime,[10] and also charting the experiences and concerns of other groups such as young people in marginalised settings as the legacy of the conflict continues to echo.[11]

When we turn to the criminal justice system, it is evident that concerns over state security shaped it from the outset. Emergency powers remained in place even when the violence of Northern Ireland's establishment subsided and no tangible or imminent emergency existed. Rather, the criminal justice system reflected the political fears of unionism, and the scale and nature of the coercive measures available stood as a bulwark against any *potential* emergency, as well as a symbolic reflection of the political complexion of the state. Through the conflict, the state's responses to paramilitary violence and large-scale disturbances involved a prioritisation of security over other considerations. This gave rise to legitimate concern that the criminal justice system was being reconstituted through the expansion and normalisation of emergency powers, and that state security concerns undermined accountability and human rights standards. As the conflict gave way to the peace process, the political transition was mirrored through a prominent police reform process and an overhaul of other elements of the criminal justice system. While some aspects of this were clearly more successful than others, one dividend of the peace process has been to cast off most of the security measures at least and reconstitute the criminal justice system in ways more attuned to the needs of its citizenry. The transitional process has also enabled innovations in respect of, for example, policing and restorative justice, and these provide valuable lessons to consider in other national contexts.

Implications and reflections

The case of Northern Ireland highlights significant aspects of the socially constructed nature of crime. In particular, it reflects the significance of politics and the state; legitimacy; and complexity and contradiction.

First, the category of 'crime' reflects a political process involving the criminalisation of particular forms of behaviour; and the state's response also involves articulating measures and powers to address it. The case of Northern Ireland highlights the role of the state within debates on crime, and particularly how definitions and responses to crime can change according to the wider socio-political environment. The 'criminalisation' policy pursued from the 1970s onwards was a prominent example of the state's expanding the scope of the criminal justice system to change how it addressed activities that hitherto had been defined and treated as 'political' in some fashion. The issue of motivation also highlights the significance of the political realm. Commitment to a particular political vision, and the organisational capacity to pursue it, can unleash levels of violence that far outstrip those arising from 'ordinary' criminality. At a collective level, political divisions in Northern Ireland caused vastly more death and destruction than crimes motivated by personal gain. Regardless of whether one viewed the claims of paramilitary organisations as valid or not – and most people did not – the motivations they articulated were the basis for their campaigns which accounted for almost 90 per cent of the fatalities arising from the conflict. In that sense, examining the relationship between crime and conflict in Northern Ireland reminds us to place the state and political frameworks of identity and solidarity centre stage if we are to have an adequate understanding of these issues.

Second, and related to the above, Northern Ireland highlights the role that legitimacy plays in the dynamics of crime and conflict. Throughout the conflict, paramilitary organisations and their members specifically claimed *not* to be ordinary criminals on the basis of their political motivation. Some sections of the population – nationalist and unionist alike – were willing to sanction or at least tolerate actions by paramilitary organisations specifically because of this.[12] Paramilitary organisations were also attentive to public opinion, and the parameters of what constituted a 'legitimate' target or operation sometimes shifted on that basis. Moreover, there was considerable public support for expanding the scope of governmental action to address paramilitary activity more robustly and decisively, including approval for 'shoot-to-kill action against terrorist suspects'[13] and collusion. Clearly, the levels of such support may be contingent on a variety of factors. Nevertheless, at various points and to varying degrees, public definitions of legitimate action encompassed crimes both by paramilitary organisations and by the state. States may be keen to view criminal definitions as fixed, but public opinion seems to accommodate the motivation behind even extreme violence – whether on the part of state or non-state actors – when reaching a judgement over its legitimacy.

Third, complexity and contradiction are evident throughout. For example, when we consider the activities of paramilitary organisations, crimes were carried out for the political purposes of attacking or defending the state, for organisational purposes such as engaging in crime for fundraising, and for social purposes such as responding to local concerns about crime through a regime (illegal, often brutal, and sometimes fatal) of paramilitary punishments. Thus, while purporting to reflect and advance the political goals of particular communities, and notwithstanding the security they claimed to provide, paramilitary organisations nevertheless acted in ways that were to the grave detriment of those communities; even at an economic level, paramilitary extortion of various businesses deterred investment in those areas and contributed to unemployment and marginalisation.[14] Paramilitary fundraising activities included the commission of crimes for which members of those communities would suffer serious punishments had they been the perpetrators; and some paramilitary members committed crimes for specifically personal purposes while operating under the name of the organisation. Similarly, the state invested enormous amounts of resources – political, financial, and flesh-and-blood costs – in combatting organisations that committed crime, while simultaneously engaging in or facilitating crime, up to and including murder, to target those organisations and to bolster state security generally. If the case of Northern Ireland confirms that illegal behaviour can form part of a state's repertoire of responses to perceived threats to state security, it especially highlights the role that state collusion with non-state actors plays in this process. Collusion is dependent on both the incentive to engage in such behaviour (and the quest for security is a powerful motivation), and the presence of organisations which can act as proxies for the state and help advance the state's goals.[15] The significance of collusion is evident not only in its direct consequences – the deaths or injuries that result from the specific actions involved – but also by its wider impact on public trust in the state and its institutions. These issues are further complicated by the opacity that tends to surround collusion as well as the high degree of immunity that its protagonists enjoy. Cumulatively, this generates a situation whereby some of the most significant dynamics of conflict can nevertheless be those least subject to scrutiny and accountability.

Others have sought to address the complexities and limitations of legalistic definitions of crime through new conceptual frameworks of 'social harm' that encompass the harms arising from corporate crime, state atrocities or other issues.[16] Here, though, the case of Northern Ireland shows that definitions of crime, responses to crime and perceptions of crime are open to contest and change, particularly in settings where the legitimacy of the state has been such a volatile and prominent backdrop.

Beyond that, the implications of Northern Ireland's history of crime, conflict and transition for other societies are complicated by the specific features of its history. While it stands as a familiar instance of a divided society – often alongside South Africa and Israel/Palestine – and a transitional process, in many ways it is a prominent but atypical example. The scale of violence, while devastating for Northern Ireland, simply does not match the ruin visited on so many other divided or war-torn societies.[17] From the mid-1970s onwards, the number of fatalities declined significantly, and thereafter one of the key features of the conflict is its duration rather than its severity.[18]

If Northern Ireland was a prominent example of a divided society characterised by sustained political violence, it also emerged as an internationally celebrated example of a peace process and a transition from conflict to relative stability. This included the establishment of new political arrangements, and particularly reforms to the criminal justice system.[19] The police reform process was especially feted as an exemplar of the shift from security-based policing to a more community-oriented model.[20] International delegations visited to witness the new policing model in action, and emissaries travelled the world to bring this success story to far-flung places. One of the key pillars of the new policing model was the robustness of its new accountability structures, including an independent police complaints system; ironically, this had been called for from the very start of the conflict, but dismissed as unwarranted. Moreover, while the new policing arrangements were highlighted for their prioritisation of 'policing with the community', much of the expertise sought by governments worldwide or transferred through training programmes or international consultancies, related to the PSNI's expertise in security policing rather than its efforts to build productive relationships with all of Northern Ireland's communities.[21]

While the principles underpinning the Patten Report reflect universal considerations regardless of the specific political environment, the relative success of the new policing landscape in Northern Ireland is bolstered by factors that do not necessarily apply in many parts of the world. For example, the transition from RUC to PSNI was enabled by – and perhaps dependent on – significant features distinguishing Northern Ireland from many other post-conflict societies.[22] These include an internationally recognised and publicly approved political settlement, shared values of governance, an established and resourced administrative infrastructure and a dynamic civil society:

> Northern Ireland is relevant to post-conflict reconstruction in what it has faced; it may be irrelevant in terms of what can be achieved. To put the point another way, if police reform requires what Northern Ireland has, then the prospects for it are bleak in all [but] one or two of the world's other trouble spots.[23]

Similarly, Ellison and Pino suggest that the level of economic investment in police reform in Northern Ireland is one of the key factors explaining its relative success, although this level of resourcing is unlikely to be available in many other societies:

There are perhaps few international lessons that Northern Ireland can offer, but if there is one it is that throwing enough money at a problem usually makes it go away or at least moderates any destabilizing impact.[24]

To raise these issues is not to diminish the successes that have occurred, and if all police forces worldwide operated under the accountability measures and human rights framework of the PSNI, that would be to humanity's great benefit.[25] Rather, my point is that perspective is crucial, and while we may laud particular features of Northern Ireland's transition and highlight innovations and practices that may have relevance for other societies – including restorative justice initiatives and policing governance – we also need to be realistic about how well or otherwise such policies may address the challenges that other jurisdictions face,[26] and indeed about the difficulties which continue to afflict other features of Northern Ireland's criminal justice system, perhaps most notably the prison system.

Running parallel to assessments of the nature and impact of the transition in Northern Ireland has been the issue of dealing with the past. Its effect on the resources of the criminal justice system, the stability of the political institutions and community relations more broadly has been immense. Much of the debate within Northern

Ireland has been on *how* the past should be addressed: through the normal criminal justice system or new bespoke mechanisms; focusing on individual cases or operating at a societal level; and oriented towards information disclosure, prosecution or reconciliation? Certainly, many societies emerging from conflict have been faced with the question of how to address the legacy of the past and the 'unspeakable truths'[27] which echo therein with South Africa's Truth and Reconciliation Commission being one of the more prominent examples of this.[28]

In recent work, David suggests that while addressing the legacy of the past is central to the dominant model of reconciliation and human rights, it is not a necessary feature of the transition from conflict to stability. Indeed, she argues that the framework of 'moral remembrance' to address the legacy of the past in societies emerging from conflict involves 'memory standardisation, institutional homogenisation and norm imitation'[29] and can be ill-attuned to the challenges faced across a wide range of contexts. She characterises 'such standardisation as being generally ineffective at best and counterproductive as worst'.[30] In the case of Northern Ireland, though, legacy issues remain a prominent feature of public and political debate. This may partly reflect the fact that there is no longer a great chasm between the economic fortunes of nationalist and unionist communities. This is *not* to dismiss or diminish the inequality that characterised Northern Ireland throughout much of its history. There were stark differentials in income and unemployment levels between those two blocs:[31] discrimination and inequality were the driving force behind the emergence of the civil rights movement in the 1960s, and in the early 1970s the Catholic unemployment rate was over 2.5 times that of Protestants. Rather, my point is that those differences have diminished markedly in the intervening years,[32] and educational participation rates are now higher for Catholics than Protestants.[33] In societies where the differences in wealth and life chances between social groups are immense and enduring, the focus in transitional periods may be on tangible measures to reduce these material disparities. In Northern Ireland, however, where the life chances of unionists and nationalists are not *vastly* different, the focus during transitional periods can fall more easily on issues of cultural rather than economic capital. The focus may be less on economic resources and more on questions of identity and recognition, including access to political power. Importantly, while seeking to address legacy issues may be a means of building or consolidating particular narratives of the conflict, and indeed of the past more generally, it also involves fundamental issues of justice and accountability. This is especially evident both in relation to the large number of unsolved murders by paramilitary organisations, and the issue of collusion and state complicity in murder.

If one key characteristic of Northern Ireland's history has been its low crime rate, another has been its political divisions. At times these divisions have been submerged beneath layers of political domination, while at others they have erupted in widespread and sustained violence. This apparently contradictory dualism of conflict and stability is one of the enduring dynamics of Northern Irish society. Writing in 2014, twenty years after the 1994 paramilitary ceasefires, Shirlow and Coulter characterised Northern Ireland as caught in 'inbetweenness':

> Northern Ireland remains snared between a whole sequence of binaries: it has edged its way from something that often felt like war toward something that does not, even yet, quite feel like peace; it exists on the fringes of the British state and at the outer limits of the peripheral vision of its Irish counterpart; it still has a unionist majority but within a generation will not; above all perhaps, it resides in the eternal antechamber – not quite British, not quite Irish – fashioned out of the competing imaginations of its principal ethno-sectarian traditions. It is these fundamental ambiguities – its quintessential 'inbetweenness' – that make Northern Ireland such a volatile political context, even twenty years after the cease-fires.[34]

As noted in the Introduction, the 'inbetweenness' of Northern Ireland is not an inherently fixed position, and demographic and socio-political changes continue to assert themselves. In addition to these internal changes, we must also take account of the influence that international factors have had on Northern Ireland's social and political landscape. The USA and EU particularly have added a significant international dimension to political developments in recent decades, not least in terms of the 1998 Belfast Agreement and EU peace and reconciliation funding programmes in the interim. Brexit may be a discordant addition to that list, but even as its impact unfolds it nevertheless highlights the influence that wider international developments can exert on Northern Ireland.

The years ahead are likely to see further significant changes to the political and social landscape of Northern Ireland. Demographic changes, a gradual shift away from some of the more traditional and fundamentalist features of its society and politics, calls for a border poll,[35] and the political and economic repercussions of Brexit will all surely exert an impact. How these will affect crime and conflict, whether they increase Northern Ireland's low crime rate or lead to further political instability and conflict, remains to be seen. For all those uncertainties, it maintains, for now, its status as a low-crime society, even as the social consequences of conflict, division and inequality reverberate through it.

Appendix: Selected Data Tables

Recorded Crime in Northern Ireland, 1923–45

Year	Number of indictable offences	Rate per 100,000 population
1923	2,599	203
1924	2,539	202
1925	2,553	203
1926	2,936	234
1927	2,668	213
1928	2,402	192
1929	2,324	187
1930	2,471	199
1931	2,753	221
1932	3,587	287
1933	3,105	247
1934	3,710	293
1935	4,350	342
1936	3,642	285
1937	3,016	235
1938	2,818	219
1939	2,579	199
1940	2,990	231
1941	3,591	279
1942	4,312	333
1943	4,569	351
1944	5,124	389
1945	5,709	433

Source: Public Record Office of Northern Ireland (PRONI) files on criminal statistics (FIN/42/1, HA/4/2/536–542, and HA/5/1389)

Selected Crimes in Northern Ireland, 1922–45

Year	Murder	Murder rate per 100,000 population	Manslaughter	Manslaughter rate per 100,000 population	Homicide (murder/ manslaughter combined rate per 100,000 population	Rape	Rape rate per 100,000 population
1922	295	23.45	14	1.11	24.56	n/a	n/a
1923	2	0.16	8	0.64	0.8	1	0.08
1924	2	0.16	2	0.16	0.32	6	0.48
1925	2	0.16	4	0.32	0.48	2	0.16
1926	3	0.24	5	0.4	0.64	2	0.16
1927	1	0.08	3	0.24	0.32	1	0.08
1928	5	0.4	11	0.88	1.28	2	0.16
1929	3	0.24	11	0.89	1.13	2	0.16
1930	2	0.16	6	0.49	0.65	5	0.4
1931	5	0.4	8	0.64	1.04	3	0.24
1932	2	0.16	4	0.32	0.48	1	0.08
1933	5	0.4	7	0.56	0.96	3	0.24
1934	5	0.4	6	0.47	0.87	2	0.16
1935	13	1.02	1	0.08	1.1	0	0
1936	1	0.08	2	0.16	0.24	3	0.23
1937	1	0.08	2	0.16	0.24	0	0
1938	2	0.16	1	0.08	0.24	8	0.62
1939	1	0.08	2	0.15	0.23	2	0.15
1940	2	0.15	3	0.23	0.38	1	0.08
1941	3	0.23	5	0.38	0.61	3	0.23
1942	8	0.6	5	0.38	0.98	3	0.23
1943	2	0.15	1	0.07	0.22	2	0.15
1944	3	0.22	3	0.22	0.44	3	0.22
1945	0	0	1	0.07	0.07	4	0.29

Source: Dane Archer and Rosemary Gartner, *Violence and Crime in Cross-National Perspective* (New Haven, CT: Yale University Press, 1984), data appendix

Recorded Crime in Northern Ireland, 1945–68

Year	Total Indictable Crime	Detection Rate (Clearup) %	Crime rate per 100,000 population	Murder	Manslaughter	Homicide (murder & manslaughter combined)	Homicide rate per 100,000 population
1945	5,709	55	433	0	1	1	0.08
1946	6,112	51	459	0	4	4	0.3
1947	6,894	44	515	0	1	1	0.08
1948	7,581	46	561	1	2	3	0.22
1949	6,241	47	459	2	2	4	0.29
1950	7,475	39	546	1	0	1	0.07
1951	8,048	43	586	0	2	2	0.15
1952	7,498	44	545	3	3	6	0.44
1953	6,890	44	498	1	2	3	0.22
1954	6,428	45 4	63	2	6	8	0.58
1955	6,049	44	434	1	0	1	0.07
1956	6,427	46	460	1	1	2	0.14
1957	6,555	45 4	69	3	1	4	0.29
1958	7,594	43	542	3	4	7	0.5
1959	7,606	45	540	0	0	0	0
1960	8,460	41	596	9	7	16	1.13
1961	9,850	37	690	5	1	6	0.42
1962	10,286	37	717	3	0	3	0.21
1963	10,859	38	751	0	0	0	0
1964	10,428	36	715	1	0	1	0.07
1965	12,846	30	874	1	0	1	0.07
1966	14,673	28	993	3	0	3	0.2
1967	15,404	29	1,033	8	1	9	0.6
1968	16,292	29	1,085	2	0	2	0.13

Source: John Brewer, Bill Lockhart and Paula Rodgers, *Crime in Ireland 1945–1995: Here be Dragons* (Oxford: Clarendon, 1997); and Northern Ireland Statistics and Research Agency.

Deaths Due to the Northern Ireland Conflict, 1969–2022

Year	RUC/PSNI (1969–2022)	Sutton (1969–2001) and Melaugh (2002–22)	McKittrick et al. (1969–2006)	Year	RUC/PSNI (1969–2022)	Sutton (1969–2001) and Melaugh (2002–22)	McKittrick et al. (1969–2006)
1969	14	16	19	1996	15	19	22
1970	25	26	29	1997	22	22	22
1971	174	171	180	1998	55	55	58
1972	470	480	496	1999	7	8	7
1973	252	255	264	2000	18	19	19
1974	220	294	304	2001	17	16	20
1975	247	260	267	2002	13	*(5) 11	11
1976	297	297	308	2003	11	(3) 10	10
1977	112	110	116	2004	5	(1) 4	4
1978	81	82	88	2005	5	(4) 8	8
1979	113	121	125	2006	3	(1) 4	3
1980	76	80	86	2007	3	(1) 3	
1981	101	114	118	2008	1	2	
1982	97	111	112	2009	5	5	
1983	77	84	87	2010	2	2	
1984	64	69	71	2011	1	1	
1985	55	57	59	2012	2	(3) 2	
1986	61	61	66	2013	1	(2) 2	
1987	95	98	106	2014	2	2	
1988	94	104	106	2015	2	(1) 3	
1989	62	76	81	2016	6	(2) 5	
1990	76	81	84	2017	2	2	
1991	94	97	102	2018	2	1	
1992	85	88	91	2019	2	(2) 1	
1993	84	88	90	2020	2	(1) 2	
1994	62	64	69	2021	2	2	
1995	9	9	9	2022	1	1	

Source: PSNI; David McKittrick, Seamus Kelters, Brian Feeney, Chris Thornton and David McVea, *Lost Lives: The stories of the men and women who died as a result of the Northern Ireland Troubles*, revised edn (London: Mainstream, 2007); and Malcolm Sutton, *An Index of Deaths from the Conflict in Northern Ireland* (2001), extended by Martin Melaugh for the period 2002–22, available at: https://cain.ulster.ac.uk/sutton/index.html. As with other data on the conflict, it important to note that these figures are compiled using different methodologies. Melaugh urges caution in relation to this data; he lists a further twenty-six deaths over the period 2002–22 in which it was uncertain whether or not they were conflict-related (these are the figures in parentheses in the table above).

Recorded Crime in Northern Ireland, 1968–1998/9

Year	Recorded Offences	Detection Rate (%)	Offences per 1,000 pop.
1968	16,292	29	11
1969	20,303	43	13
1970	24,810	41	16
1971	30,828	32	20
1972	35,884	21	23
1973	32,057	28	21
1974	33,314	29	22
1975	37,234	21	24
1976	39,779	24	26
1977	45,335	22	29
1978	45,335	23	29
1979	54,262	21	35
1980	56,316	26	37
1981	62,496	27	41
1982	62,020	19	40
1983	63,984	28	41
1984	66,779	31	43
1985	64,584	35	41
1986	68,255	37	43
1987	63,860	43	40
1988	55,890	45	35
1989	55,147	43	35
1990	57,198	38	36
1991	63,492	36	40
1992	67,532	34	42
1993	66,228	36	40
1994	67,886	36	41
1995	68,808	36	42
1996	68,549	34	41
1997	62,222	31	37
1997/98	59,922	32	36
1998/99	76,644	27	46
1998/99 (new rules)	109,053	29	65

Source: John Brewer, Bill Lockhart and Paula Rodgers, *Crime in Ireland 1945–1995: Here be Dragons* (Oxford: Oxford University Press, 1997), and RUC. A new system of recording crime (the 'counting rules') was established on 1 April 1998. The two sets of figures for 1998/99 include those generated under the 'old' rules (in place up until 31 March 1998) as well as under the 'new' rules.

Homicide in Northern Ireland, 1969–2019

Year	Murder	Manslaughter	Infanticide	Corporate Manslaughter	Homicide	Rate per 100,000 pop.
1969	5	8			13	0.86
1970	14	6			20	1.31
1971	123	21			144	9.39
1972	376	17			393	25.54
1973	200	15			215	14.05
1974	205	8			213	13.95
1975	238	9			247	16.21
1976	280	11			291	19.10
1977	116	5	2		123	8.07
1978	82	2	1		85	5.58
1979	128	7	1		136	8.90
1980	85	5	3		93	6.07
1981	95	7	0		102	6.61
1982	99	5	0		104	6.73
1983	86	4	1		91	5.87
1984	63	2	0		65	4.17
1985	59	2	0		61	3.90
1986	85	2	0		87	5.53
1987	100	6	3		109	6.89
1988	111	5	0		116	7.32
1989	67	8	0		75	4.72
1990	71	11	0		82	5.14
1991	114	7	0		121	7.53
1992	108	3	0		111	6.84
1993	101	5	0		106	6.48
1994	82	3	1		86	5.23
1995	22	1	1		24	1.46
1996	35	4	0		39	2.35
1997	40	2	0		42	2.51
1998	80	1	0		81	4.83
1999	29	8	0		37	2.20
2000	42	3	0		45	2.67
2001	53	4	0		57	3.37
2002	35	3	0		38	2.24
2003	35	6	1		42	2.46
2004	30	4	0		34	1.98
2005	26	3	2		31	1.79
2006	27	3	0		30	1.72
2007	26	3	0		29	1.65
2008	20	4	0	0	24	1.35
2009	25	4	0	0	29	1.62
2010	15	8	0	0	23	1.27
2011	17	5	0	2	24	1.32
2012	17	4	0	0	21	1.15
2013	19	1	0	1	21	1.15
2014	13	4	0	4	21	1.14
2015	20	3	0	0	23	1.24
2016	17	2	0	0	19	1.02
2017	18	6	0	0	24	1.28
2018	21	2	0	1	24	1.28
2019	25	4	0	0	29	1.53

Source: Homicide figures from PSNI, and population estimates from National Ireland
Statistics and Research Agency.

Paramilitary Punishments in Northern Ireland, 1973–98

Year	Loyalist Shootings	Loyalist Assaults	Loyalist Total	Republican Shootings	Republican Assaults	Republican Total	Total overall
1973	21		21	53		53	74
1974	43		43	84		84	127
1975	50		50	139		139	189
1976	36		36	62		62	98
1977	28		28	98		98	126
1978	17		17	50		50	67
1979	25		25	51		51	76
1980	26		26	51		51	77
1981	14		14	66		66	80
1982	22		22	59		59	81
1983	9		9	22		22	31
1984	6		6	20		20	26
1985	11		11	21		21	32
1986	24		24	17		17	41
1987	67		67	57		57	124
1988	34	21	55	32	35	67	122
1989	65	23	88	96	28	124	212
1990	60	21	81	46	47	93	174
1991	40	22	62	36	40	76	138
1992	72	36	108	61	38	99	207
1993	60	35	95	25	6	31	126
1994	68	38	106	54	32	86	192
1995	3	76	79	0	141	141	220
1996	21	130	151	3	172	175	326
1997	46	78	124	26	78	104	228
1998	34	89	123	38	55	93	216
Total	902	569	1,471	1,267	672	1,939	3,410

Source: RUC/PSNI. Note the RUC did not report figures for paramilitary *shootings* until 1973 and *assaults* until 1988.

Public Attitudes to the Police in Northern Ireland, 2007–18

Year	Performance of local police		Performance of PSNI in Northern Ireland as a whole		Satisfaction that PSNI treat members of the public fairly in Northern Ireland as a whole	
	% responding 'very/fairly good'		% responding 'very/fairly good'		% responding 'very/fairly satisfied'	
	Catholic	Protestant	Catholic	Protestant	Catholic	Protestant
2007 (Oct)	54	67	62	71	62	73
2008 (April)	56	60	65	66	68	73
2008 (Sept)	59	64	66	71	63	75
2009 (April)	59	69	67	79	64	78
2009 (Sept)	55	57	61	65	66	75
2010 (Sept)	57	61	62	73	61	74
2012 (Jan)	54	64	63	73	62	74
2013 (Jan)	64	67	63	76	67	80
2014 (Jan)	65	69	70	73	68	77
2015 (Jan)	66	67	66	73	67	71
2016 (April)	64	73	68	81	66	77
2017 (April)	73	76	76	84	73	85
2018 (May)	65	71	--	--	68	81

Source: Northern Ireland Policing Board Omnibus Surveys, 2007–18, available at: https://www.nipolicingboard.org.uk/surveys.

Recorded Crime in Northern Ireland, 1998/9–2022/3

Year	Total recorded crime (excluding fraud)	Rate of recorded crime (excluding fraud) per 1,000 pop.	Total recorded fraud offences	Total recorded crime (including fraud)	Rate of recorded crime (including fraud) per 1,000 pop.
1998/9	104,647	62	4,406	109,053	65
1999/2000	114,209	68	4,902	119,111	71
2000/1	115,791	69	4,122	119,912	71
2001/2	135,814	80	3,972	139,786	83
2002/3	138,132	81	4,346	142,496	84
2003/4	124,966	73	2,987	127,953	75
2004/5	115,965	68	2,159	118,124	69
2005/6	120,919	70	2,275	123,194	71
2006/7	119,314	68	1,830	121,144	69
2007/8	107,490	61	978	108,468	62
2008/9	108,870	61	1,224	110,094	62
2009/10	107,951	60	1,188	109,139	61
2010/11	103,676	57	1,364	105,040	58
2011/12	102,009	56	1,380	103,389	57
2012/13	98,558	54	1,831	100,389	55
2013/14	100,917	55	1,829	102,746	56
2014/15	103,176	56	1,896	105,072	57
2015/16	104,926	57	2,230	107,156	58
2016/17	98,006	53	3,163	101,169	54
2017/18	98,105	52	3,592	101,697	54
2018/19	100,854	54	3,608	104,462	56
2019/20	106,492	56	4,253	110,745	59
2020/1	94,231	50	5,856	100,195	53
2021/2	106,621	56	5,464	112,085	59
2022/3	111,571	59	4,671	116,242	61

Source: PSNI

Crime Victimisation Rates in Northern Ireland, 1998–2021/2

Year	Victimisation Rate (%)
1998	23.0
2001	19.7
2003/4	21.4
2005	17.3
2006/7	14.2
2007/8	13.8
2008/9	13.4
2009/10	14.3
2010/11	12.6
2011/12	11.2
2012/13	10.9
2013/14	10.0
2014/15	8.8
2015/16	8.9
2016/17	8.7
2017/18	7.9
2018/19	7.5
2019/20	6.9
2020/1	3.9
2021/2	3.8

Source: P. Campbell, A. Rice and K. Ross, *Experience of Crime: Findings from the 2019/20 Northern Ireland Safe Community Survey* (Belfast: Department of Justice, 2021); and K. Ross and M. Beggs, *Experience of Crime and Perceptions of Crime and Policing and Justice: Findings from the 2021/22 Northern Ireland Safe Community Telephone Survey* (Belfast: Department of Justice, 2023). Note: because of the Covid-19 pandemic, different methodologies were used in 2020/1 and 2021/2 (interviews were conducted by telephone rather than face-to-face), and so the results are not directly comparable with previous surveys.

Paramilitary Punishments (Shootings and Assaults), 1998/9–2022/3

	Loyalist			Republican			Total
	Shootings	Assaults	Total	Shootings	Assaults	Total	Overall
1998/9	40	112	152	33	60	93	245
1999/2000	53	70	123	22	33	55	178
2000/1	99	89	188	63	72	135	323
2001/2	124	76	200	66	36	102	302
2002/3	110	94	204	55	50	105	309
2003/4	102	101	203	47	48	95	298
2004/5	76	71	147	17	45	62	209
2005/6	70	57	127	6	19	25	152
2006/7	14	36	50	12	12	24	74
2007/8	2	35	37	5	10	15	52
2008/9	2	28	30	18	13	31	61
2009/10	1	69	70	45	12	57	127
2010/11	0	34	34	33	16	49	83
2011/12	0	31	31	33	15	48	79
2012/13	1	27	28	26	9	35	63
2013/14	9	37	46	19	5	24	70
2014/15	6	42	48	30	16	46	94
2015/16	1	47	48	13	11	24	72
2016/17	3	56	59	25	10	35	94
2017/18	1	50	51	21	15	36	87
2018/19	2	45	47	17	14	31	78
2019/20	2	48	50	11	19	30	80
2020/1	4	31	35	14	8	22	57
2021/2	7	30	37	5	3	8	45
2022/3	4	23	27	7	9	16	43
TOTAL	733	1,339	2,072	643	560	1,203	3,275

Source: PSNI

Notes

All URL links are valid at time of publication.

INTRODUCTION

1. Jennifer Todd, *Identity Change after Conflict* (London: Palgrave Macmillan, 2018).

2. Results of the 2021 census are available at: https://www.nisra.gov.uk/statistics/2021-census/results/main-statistics.

3. Further details of the survey results are available at: https://www.ark.ac.uk/nilt/2021/.

4. John Whyte, *Interpreting Northern Ireland* (Oxford: Oxford University Press, 1990), p. viii.

5. Adrian Guelke, *Politics in Deeply Divided Societies* (Cambridge: Polity, 2012); Frank Wright, *Northern Ireland: A comparative analysis* (Dublin: Gill & Macmillan, 1987).

6. See, for example, Monica McWilliams and Fionnuala Ní Aoláin, '"There Is A War Going On, You Know": Addressing the complexity of violence against women in conflicted and post conflict societies', *Transitional Justice Review*, vol. 1, no. 2, 2013, pp. 4–44; Graham Ellison and Nathan Pino, *Globalisation, Development and Security Sector Reform* (London: Macmillan, 2012); and Rachel Monaghan, 'Community-based Justice in Northern Ireland and South Africa', *International Criminal Justice Review*, vol. 18, no. 1, 2008, pp. 83–105.

7. While conflict is often equated with overt violence, the reality is that 'stability' tends to be a key dynamic of conflicts. Even in highly violent contexts, violence occurs sporadically and most people do not directly participate in violence. See, generally, Randall Collins, *Violence: A micro-sociological theory* (Princeton: Princeton University Press, 2008); and Siniša Malešević, *Why Humans Fight: The social dynamics of close-range violence* (Cambridge: Cambridge University Press, 2022).

8. Brendan O'Leary, *A Treatise on Northern Ireland, Volume III: Consociation and Confederation* (Oxford: Oxford University Press, 2019), p. xli.

9. Whyte, *Interpreting Northern Ireland*, p. xi.

10. Her full speech is available at: https://www.margaretthatcher.org/document/104589.

11. Kieran McEvoy, *Paramilitary Imprisonment in Northern Ireland* (Oxford: Oxford University Press, 2001), p. 6.

12. See, for example, Brian Hanley, *Republicanism, Crime and Paramilitary Policing, 1916–2020* (Cork: Cork University Press, 2022).

13. Northern Ireland Affairs Committee, *Organised Crime in Northern Ireland* (London: Stationery Office, 2006), p. 11.

14. Bill Rolston and Mike Tomlinson, 'Spectators at the "Carnival of Reaction"? Analysing political crime in Northern Ireland', in Mary Kelly, Liam O'Dowd and James Wickham (eds), *Power, Conflict and Inequality* (Dublin: Turoe Press, 1982), p. 25.

15. John Brewer, Bill Lockhart and Paula Rodgers, *Crime in Ireland 1945–1995: Here be Dragons* (Oxford: Oxford University Press, 1997), p. 4.

16. Ken Pease and Mike Morrissey, 'The Importance of Northern Ireland for Criminal Justice Research in Great Britain', *Howard Journal of Criminal Justice*, vol. 21, no. 3, 1982, p. 136.

17. Ibid., p. 134.

18. Tony Jefferson and Joanna Shapland, 'Criminal Justice and the Production of Order and Control: Criminological research in the UK in the 1980s', *British Journal of Criminology*, vol. 34, no. 3, 1994, p. 281.

19. David Downes and Rod Morgan, 'Dumping the "Hostages to Fortune"? The politics of law and order in Britain', in Mike Maguire, Rod Morgan and Robert Reiner (eds), *Oxford Handbook of Criminology*, 3rd edn (Oxford: Oxford University Press, 2002), p. 315.

20. Kieran McEvoy, Ron Dudai and Cheryl Lawther, 'Criminology and Transitional Justice', in Alison Liebling, Shadd Maruna and Lesley McAra (eds), *Oxford Handbook of Criminology*, 6th edn (Oxford: Oxford University Press, 2017).

21. Brewer et al., *Crime in Ireland 1945–1995*.

22. Some topics, such as prostitution and sex work generally, received little attention, although that has changed in recent years. For analyses of historical and contemporary dimensions of sex work, see Leanne McCormick, *Regulating Sexuality: Women in twentieth-century Northern Ireland* (Manchester: Manchester University Press, 2009); and Graham Ellison, 'Criminalizing the Payment for Sex in Northern Ireland: Sketching the contours of a moral panic', *British Journal of Criminology*, vol. 57, no. 1, 2017, pp. 194–214.

23. See, for example, Nicola Carr, 'The Criminal Justice System in Northern Ireland', in Steve Case, Phil Johnson, David Manlow, Roger Smith and Kate Williams (eds), *Criminology* (Oxford: Oxford University Press, 2017); and Graham Ellison and Aogán Mulcahy, 'Crime and Criminal Justice in Northern Ireland', in Anthea Hucklesby and Azrini Wahidin (eds), *Criminal Justice* (Oxford: Oxford University Press, 2009).

24. Brewer et al., *Crime in Ireland 1945–1995*; Deirdre Healy, Claire Hamilton, Yvonne Daly and Michelle Butler (eds), *Routledge Handbook of Irish Criminology* (London: Routledge, 2016).

25. Paddy Hillyard, 'Lessons from Ireland', in Bob Fine and Robert Millar (eds), *Policing the Miners' Strike* (London: Lawrence & Wishart, 1985); Paddy Hillyard, 'The Normalisation of Special Powers', in Phil Scraton (ed.), *Law, Order and the Authoritarian State* (Milton Keynes: Open University Press, 1987); Mike Tomlinson, 'Policing the New Europe: The Northern Ireland factor', in Tony Bunyan (ed.), *Statewatching the New Europe* (London: Statewatch, 1993); Mike Tomlinson, 'Imprisoned Ireland', in Vincenzo Ruggiero, Mike Ryan and Joe Sim (eds), *Western European Penal Systems* (London: Sage, 2005); see also Aogán Mulcahy, 'The "Other" Lessons from Ireland? Policing, political violence and policy transfer', *European Journal of Criminology*, vol. 2, no. 2, 2005, pp. 185–209.

26. My discussion here is far from exhaustive, but for excellent overviews see Kieran McEvoy and Graham Ellison, 'Criminological Discourses in Northern Ireland: Conflict and conflict resolution', in Kieran McEvoy and Tim Newburn (eds), *Criminology, Conflict Resolution and Restorative Justice* (New York: Palgrave Macmillan,

2003); and Anne-Marie McAlinden and Clare Dwyer (eds), *Criminal Justice in Transition: The Northern Ireland context* (Oxford: Hart, 2015).

27. Mary Corcoran, *Out of Order: The political imprisonment of women in Northern Ireland 1972–1998* (Cullompton: Willan, 2006); McEvoy, *Paramilitary Imprisonment in Northern Ireland*; Linda Moore and Phil Scraton, *The Incarceration of Women: Punishing bodies, breaking spirits* (Basingstoke: Palgrave Macmillan, 2014).

28. John Brewer with Kathleen Magee, *Inside the RUC: Routine policing in a divided society* (Oxford: Clarendon, 1991); Graham Ellison and Jim Smyth, *The Crowned Harp: Policing Northern Ireland* (London: Pluto, 2000); Aogán Mulcahy, *Policing Northern Ireland: Conflict, legitimacy and reform* (Cullompton: Willan, 2006); Mary O'Rawe, 'Transitional Policing Arrangements in Northern Ireland: The can't and the won't of the change dialectic', *Fordham International Law Journal*, vol. 26, no. 4, 2003, pp. 1015–73; John Topping, 'Community Policing in Northern Ireland: A resistance narrative', *Policing and Society*, vol. 18, no. 4, 2008, pp. 377–96; Ronald Weitzer, *Policing Under Fire: Ethnic conflict and police–community relations in Northern Ireland* (Albany: SUNY, 1995).

29. Brewer et al., *Crime in Ireland 1945–1995*; Brian Caul, John Pinkerton and Fred Powell (eds), *The Juvenile Justice System in Northern Ireland* (Newtownabbey: Ulster Polytechnic, 1983); David O'Mahony, Ray Geary, Kieran McEvoy and John Morison, *Crime, Community and Locale: The Northern Ireland Communities Crime Survey* (Aldershot: Ashgate, 2000).

30. McWilliams and Ní Aoláin, '"There Is A War Going On, You Know"'.

31. Heather Hamill, *The Hoods: Crime and punishment in Belfast* (Princeton, NJ: Princeton University Press, 2011); Dave McCullough, Tanja Schmidt and Bill Lockhart, *Car Theft in Northern Ireland: Recent studies on a persistent problem* (Belfast: Extern, 1990); and Sean O'Connell, 'Emotional Journeys: Belfast and the oral history of joyriding', *Oral History*, vol. 51, no. 1, 2023, pp. 59–69.

32. McAlinden and Dwyer (eds), *Criminal Justice in Transition*.

33. Brewer et al., *Crime in Ireland 1945–1995*, p. 4.

34. For overviews, see Brewer et al., *Crime in Ireland 1945–1995*; John Brewer, Bill Lockhart and Paula Rodgers, 'Informal Social Control and Crime Management in Belfast', *British Journal of Sociology*, vol. 49, no. 4, 1998, pp. 570–85; Healy et al., *Routledge Handbook of Irish Criminology*; McAlinden and Dwyer, *Criminal Justice in Transition*; and McEvoy and Ellison, 'Criminological Discourses in Northern Ireland'.

35. Edwin Sutherland, Bill Cressey and David Luckenbill, *Principles of Criminology*, 11th edn (Lanham, MD: General Hall, 1992), p. 3.

36. David Matza, *Becoming Deviant* (Englewood Cliffs, NJ: Prentice Hall, 1969), p. 143.

37. Stan Cohen, 'Crime and Politics: Spot the difference', *British Journal of Sociology*, vol. 47, no. 1, 1996, pp. 1–21.

38. For an overview, see Russell Hogg and Kerry Carrington (eds), *Critical Criminology* (Cullompton: Willan, 2002).

39. Ross McGarry and Sandra Walklate, 'Introduction', in Sandra Walklate and Ross McGarry (eds), *Criminology and War: Transgressing the borders* (Abingdon: Routledge, 2015), p. 2.

40. Susan Karstedt and Gary LaFree, 'Democracy, Crime and Justice', *Annals of the American Academy of Political and Social Science*, vol. 605, no. 1, 2006, pp. 6–23.

41. Ruth Jamieson (ed), *The Criminology of War* (Abingdon: Routledge, 2016), p. xiii.

42. Wright, *Northern Ireland*, pp. 180–1.

43. Much of this literature is particularly attentive to the impact that conflict or transitional contexts have for the emergence of organised crime, and/or by paramilitary groups morphing into criminal groups as conflicts end. See, for example, John de Boer and Louise Bosetti, *The Crime-Conflict 'Nexus': State of the evidence*, United Nations University Centre for Policy Research, Occasional Paper 5; José Gutiérrez and Frances Thomson, 'Rebels-Turned-Narcos? The

FARC-EP's political involvement in Colombia's cocaine economy', *Studies in Conflict & Terrorism*, vol. 44, no. 1, 2020, pp. 26–51; Tamara Makarenko, 'The Crime-Terror Continuum: Tracing the interplay between transnational organised crime and terrorism', *Global Crime*, vol. 6, no. 1, 2004, pp. 129–45; Christina Steenkamp, 'The Crime-Conflict Nexus and the Civil War in Syria', *Stability: International journal of security & development*, vol. 6, no. 1, 2017, pp. 1–18.

44. Katja Aas, *Globalisation and Crime*, 2nd edn (London: Sage, 2019); David Nelken, *Comparative Criminal Justice* (London: Sage, 2010).

45. See, for example, Kerry Carrington, Russell Hogg, John Scott and Maximo Sozzo (eds), *The Palgrave Handbook of Criminology and the Global South* (London: Palgrave Macmillan, 2018).

46. The data presented here are taken from: https://ourworldindata. org/grapher/countries-democracies-autocracies-row. Various organisations that monitor these issues use slightly different definitions, but the broad trends they report are very closely aligned. See also, for example, *The Economist*'s 'Democracy Index' and the Fund for Peace's 'Fragile States Index'.

47. Håvard Strand and Håvard Hegre, 'Trends in Armed Conflict, 1946–2020', *Conflict Trends*, vol. 3, no. 1, 2021.

48. United Nations Development Programme, *Human Development Report 1994: New dimensions of human security* (Geneva: United Nations, 1994), p. 1, available at: http://www.hdr.undp.org/en/ content/human-development-report-1994.

49. See, generally, Mary Martin and Taylor Owen (eds), *Routledge Handbook of Human Security* (London: Routledge, 2013).

50. David Bayley, *Changing the Guard: Developing democratic policing abroad* (Oxford: Oxford University Press, 2006); Ellison and Pino, *Globalisation*.

51. United Nations Sustainable Development Goals, available at: https://sdgs.un.org/.

52. Jarrett Blaustein, Nathan Pino, Kate Fitz-Gibbon and Rob White, 'Criminology and the UN Sustainable Development Goals: The need

for support and critique', *British Journal of Criminology*, vol. 58, no. 4, 2018, pp. 767–86.

53. Mercedes Hinton and Tim Newburn (eds), *Policing Developing Democracies* (London: Routledge, 2009).

54. Benoit Dupont, Peter Grabosky and Clifford Shearing, 'The Governance of Security in Weak and Failing States', *Criminal Justice*, vol. 3, no. 4, 2003, p. 332.

55. John Braithwaite, 'Crime as a Cascade Phenomenon', *International Journal of Comparative and Applied Criminal Justice*, vol. 44, no. 3, 2020, pp. 137–69.

56. Louise Shelley, *Dirty Entanglements: Corruption, crime and terrorism* (Cambridge: Cambridge University Press, 2014).

57. Anna Funder, *Stasiland* (London: Granta Books, 2004); John Koehler, *Stasi: The untold story of the East German secret police* (New York: Basic Books, 2000).

58. David Shearer, *Policing Stalin's Socialism: Repression and social order in the Soviet Union, 1924–1953* (New Haven, CT: Yale University Press, 2009); Louise Shelley, *Policing Soviet Society: The evolution of state control* (London: Routledge, 2005); George Browder, *Foundations of the Nazi Police State: The formation of Sipo and SD* (Kentucky: University Press of Kentucky, 2004).

59. Brewer et al., 'Informal Social Control'.

60. Mark Shaw, 'Crime, Police and Public in Transitional Societies', *Transformation*, vol. 49, no. 1, 2002, pp. 1–24.

61. Gary LaFree and Andromachi Tseloni, 'Democracy and Crime: A multilevel analysis of homicide trends in forty-four countries, 1950–2000', *Annals of the American Academy of Political and Social Science*, vol. 605, no. 1, 2006, pp. 26–49.

62. Christina Steenkamp, 'In the Shadows of War and Peace: Making sense of violence after peace accords', *Conflict, Security and Development*, vol. 11, no. 3, 2011, p. 378.

63. Roger Mac Ginty, *No War, No Peace: The rejuvenation of stalled peace processes and peace accords* (Basingstoke: Palgrave Macmillan, 2006).

64. Priscilla Hayner, *Unspeakable Truths: Transitional justice and the challenge of truth commissions*, 2nd edn (London: Routledge, 2010).

65. Mike Brogden and Clifford Shearing, *Policing for a New South Africa* (London: Routledge, 1993); Monique Marks, *Transforming the Robocops: Changing police in South Africa* (Durban: University of KwaZulu-Natal Press, 2005).

66. Kieran McEvoy and Lorna McGregor (eds), *Transitional Justice from Below: Grassroots activism and the struggle for change* (New York: Bloomsbury Publishing, 2008).

CHAPTER 1: STABILITY: 1920–68

1. For different perspectives on the establishment of Northern Ireland and its social and political dynamics, see Paul Bew, Peter Gibbon and Henry Patterson, *Northern Ireland 1921–2001: Political forces and social classes* (London: Serif, 2002); Patrick Buckland, *The Factory of Grievances: Devolved government in Northern Ireland, 1921–39* (Dublin: Gill & Macmillan, 1979); Michael Farrell, *Northern Ireland: The Orange state*, 2nd edn (London: Pluto, 1980); Bryan Follis, *A State Under Siege: The establishment of Northern Ireland 1920–1925* (Oxford: Clarendon, 1995); John McGarry and Brendan O'Leary, *Explaining Northern Ireland: Broken images* (Oxford: Blackwell, 1995); Liam O'Dowd, Bill Rolston and Mike Tomlinson, *Northern Ireland: Between civil rights and civil war* (London: CSE Books, 1980); Brendan O'Leary and John McGarry, *Understanding Northern Ireland: The politics of antagonism* (London: Athlone, 1996); Joe Ruane and Jennifer Todd, *The Dynamics of Conflict in Northern Ireland: Power, conflict and emancipation* (Cambridge: Cambridge University Press, 1996); and John Whyte, *Interpreting Northern Ireland* (Oxford: Oxford University Press, 1990).

2. The 1911 Census of Ireland indicates the respective percentages of Protestants and Catholics in Northern Ireland's six constituent counties as: Antrim, 79.5 and 20.5; Down, 68.4 and 31.6; Derry, 58.5 and 41.5; Armagh, 54.7 and 45.3; Tyrone, 44.6 and 55.4; and Fermanagh, 43.8 and 56.2. See Farrell, *Northern Ireland*, p. viii.

3. Ruane and Todd, *The Dynamics of Conflict in Northern Ireland*.

4. Bew et al., *Northern Ireland 1921–2001*; O'Leary and McGarry, *Understanding Northern Ireland*; Ruane and Todd, *The Dynamics of Conflict in Northern Ireland*; John Whyte, 'How Much Discrimination Was There under the Unionist Regime, 1921–1968?', in Tom Gallagher and James O'Connell (eds), *Contemporary Irish Studies* (Manchester: Manchester University Press, 1983).

5. O'Leary and McGarry, *Understanding Northern Ireland*, p. 107.

6. Richard Rose, *Governing Without Consensus* (London: Faber & Faber, 1971).

7. Alan Parkinson, *Belfast's Unholy Wars: The Troubles of the 1920s* (Dublin: Four Courts Press, 2004), p. 12. See also Robert Lynch, *The Partition of Ireland, 1918–1925* (Cambridge: Cambridge University Press, 2019).

8. Niall Cunningham, '"The Doctrine of Vicarious Punishment": Space, religion and the Belfast Troubles of 1920–22', *Journal of Historical Geography*, vol. 40, no. 1, 2013, p. 52.

9. Parkinson, *Belfast's Unholy Wars*.

10. Tim Wilson, '"The Most Terrible Assassination That Has Yet Stained the Name of Belfast": The McMahon murders in context', *Irish Historical Studies*, vol. 37, no. 145, 2010, pp. 83–106.

11. Ibid., p. 86.

12. Parkinson, *Belfast's Unholy Wars*, pp. 236–9. See also Michael Farrell, *Arming the Protestants: The formation of the Ulster Special Constabulary and the Royal Ulster Constabulary 1920–27* (Dingle: Brandon Books, 1983).

13. Jonathan Bardon, *A History of Ulster* (Belfast: Blackstaff, 1992), p. 494.

14. Fearghal McGarry, 'Revolution, 1916–1923', in Thomas Bartlett (ed.), *Cambridge History of Ireland*, vol. 4 (Cambridge: Cambridge University Press, 2018), p. 283.

15. Cunningham, '"The Doctrine of Vicarious Punishment"'.

16. Wilson, '"The Most Terrible Assassination That Has Yet Stained the Name of Belfast"', p. 89.

17. Bardon, *A History of Ulster*.

18. Quoted in Farrell, *Northern Ireland*, p. 221.

19. Bardon, *A History of Ulster*, 495.

20. O'Leary and McGarry, *Understanding Northern Ireland*.

21. Ruane and Todd, *The Dynamics of Conflict in Northern Ireland*, p. 131; Neville Douglas, 'Political Structures, Social Interaction and Identity Change in Northern Ireland', in Brian Graham (ed.), *In Search of Ireland: A cultural geography* (London: Routledge, 1997), p. 156.

22. Northern Ireland was certainly not the only state to be preoccupied with issues of security. For a discussion of the role that security concerns played in a variety of national contexts, and of the range of counter-insurgency measures employed, see David French, *The British Way in Counter-Insurgency, 1945–1967* (Oxford: Oxford University Press, 2011). For further analysis of these issues in the specific context of the establishment of Northern Ireland, see Farrell, *Arming the Protestants*; and Follis, *A State Under Siege*.

23. Ronald Weitzer, *Policing Under Fire: Ethnic conflict and police–community relations in Northern Ireland* (Albany: SUNY, 1995), p. 34. In the Free State in 1926, following the amalgamation of An Garda Síochána with the Dublin Metropolitan Police, the establishment strength was set at 7,206 officers, giving a police–public ratio of 1:412. See Liam McNiffe, *A History of the Garda Síochána* (Dublin: Wolfhound, 1997), p. 65.

24. Graham Ellison and Jim Smyth, *The Crowned Harp: Policing Northern Ireland* (London: Pluto, 2000); and Aogán Mulcahy, *Policing Northern Ireland: Conflict, legitimacy and reform* (Cullompton: Willan, 2006).

25. Farrell, *Northern Ireland*, p. 50.

26. Hunt Committee, *Report of the Advisory Committee on Police in Northern Ireland*, Cmd. 535 (London: Stationery Office, 1969), p. 21.

27. Ibid., p. 40.

28. https://hudsonreview.com/1983/07/station-island/

29. Christopher Magill, *Political Conflict in East Ulster: Revolution and reprisal* (Woodbridge: Boydell, 2020), p. 174.

30. Rosemary Harris, *Prejudice and Tolerance in Ulster: A study of neighbours and 'strangers' in a border community*, 2nd edn (Manchester: Manchester University Press, 1986), pp. 180–1.

31. Scarman Tribunal, *Violence and Civil Disturbances in Northern Ireland in 1969: Report of tribunal of inquiry*, Cmd 566 (Belfast: Stationery Office, 1972), p. 17.

32. For starkly contrasting views on the B-Specials, see Farrell, 1983, *Arming the Protestants*, and Sir Arthur Hezlet, *The 'B' Specials: A history of the Ulster Special Constabulary* (London: Tom Stacey, 1972). For a more recent and less polarised account, see Magill, *Political Conflict in East Ulster*.

33. Quoted in Farrell, *Northern Ireland*, pp. 93–4.

34. While the British government has indicated its willingness to step in and enact legislation broadening Northern Ireland's access to abortion, this has been the subject of ongoing dispute in relation to the resourcing of clinics and political opposition from some parties within Northern Ireland. See, for example, https://www.bbc.com/news/uk-northern-ireland-politics-56041849.

35. Rose, *Governing Without Consensus*, p. 248.

36. Yves Lambert, 'A Turning Point in Religious Evolution in Europe', *Journal of Contemporary Religion*, vol. 19, no. 1, 2004, pp. 29–45.

37. Claire Mitchell, *Religion, Identity and Belonging in Northern Ireland: Boundaries of belonging and belief* (Farnham: Ashgate, 2006), p. 26.

38. Donald Akenson, *Small Differences: Irish Catholics and Irish Protestants, 1815–1922* (Dublin: Gill & Macmillan, 1988).

39. This stability was also characteristic of nineteenth-century Ireland. Although uprisings and violence were recurring features of the 1800s, these periods of conflict were sandwiched between

longer periods of relative calm. This is not to downplay the tensions, grievances and undercurrents of hostility that characterised relations between Catholic and Protestant groups (and the repeated recourse to emergency measures) – particularly in relation to struggles over land ownership and the living conditions of tenant farmers. Rather, my aim is simply to note that violence was only part of the way in which these were played out, and much of the violence that did occur was unrelated to sectarian or political tensions. For analyses of different aspects of these social dynamics, see Akenson, *Small Differences*; Richard Mc Mahon, *Homicide in Pre-Famine and Famine Ireland* (Liverpool: Liverpool University Press, 2013); Charles Townsend, *Political Violence in Ireland: Government and resistance since 1848* (Oxford: Clarendon, 1983); and William Vaughan, *Landlords and Tenants in Mid-Victorian Ireland* (Oxford: Oxford University Press, 1994).

40. Graham McFarlane, '"It's Not as Simple as That": The expression of the Catholic and Protestant boundary in Northern Irish rural communities', in Anthony Cohen (ed.), *Symbolising Boundaries: Identity and diversity in British cultures* (Manchester: Manchester University Press, 1986), pp. 92–3.

41. Ibid., p. 93.

42. Harris, *Prejudice and Tolerance in Ulster*, p. 185.

43. Akenson, *Small Differences*, p. 149.

44. Harris, *Prejudice and Tolerance in Ulster*, p. ix.

45. The full text is available at: https://allpoetry.com/ poem/11014161-from-Whatever-You-Say-Say-Nothing-by-Seamus-Heaney.

46. Mixed marriages were relatively rare in Ireland, particularly in Ulster. The 1911 census indicated that marriages between Catholics and members of other religions comprised less than 1 per cent of total marriages. See Alan Fernihough, Cormac Ó Gráda and Brendan Walsh, 'Intermarriage in a Divided Society: Ireland a century ago', *Explorations in Economic History*, vol. 56, no. 1, 2015, pp. 1–14.

47. Frank Burton, *The Politics of Legitimacy: Struggles in a Belfast community* (London: Routledge & Kegan Paul, 1978).

48. John Darby, *Intimidation and the Control of Conflict in Northern Ireland* (Dublin: Gill & Macmillan, 1986), p. 20.

49. Frederick Boal and Neville Douglas (eds), *Integration and Division: Geographical perspectives on the Northern Ireland problem* (London: Academic Press, 1982); Darby, *Intimidation and the Control of Conflict in Northern Ireland*.

50. See, generally, Mark Finnane, 'A Decline in Violence in Ireland? Crime, policing and social relations, 1860–1914', *Crime, Histoire et Sociétés/Crime, History and Societies*, vol. 1, no. 1, 1997, pp. 51–70; Mark Finnane and Ian O'Donnell, 'Crime and Punishment', in Eugenia Bagini and Mary Daly (eds), *The Cambridge Social History of Modern Ireland* (Cambridge: Cambridge University Press, 2017); Mark Radford, *The Policing of Belfast 1870–1914* (London: Bloomsbury, 2015); and Townsend, *Political Violence in Ireland*.

51. Jonathan Bardon, *A History of Ireland in 250 Episodes* (Dublin: Gill & Macmillan, 2008), p. 478.

52. Dane Archer and Rosemary Gartner, *Violence and Crime in Cross-National Perspective* (New Haven, CT: Yale University Press, 1984).

53. Manuel Eisner, 'Modernization, Self-Control and Lethal Violence: The long-term dynamics of European homicide rates in theoretical perspective', *British Journal of Criminology*, vol. 41, no. 4, 2001, pp. 618–38; Ted Gurr, 'Historical Trends in Violent Crime: A critical review of the evidence', *Crime and Justice*, vol. 3, 1981, pp. 295–353.

54. Tim Wilson, *Frontiers of Violence: Conflict and identity in Ulster and Upper Silesia 1918–1922* (Oxford: Oxford University Press, 2010), p. 166.

55. Archer and Gartner, *Violence and Crime in Cross-National Perspective*.

56. Nial Osborough, *Borstal in Ireland: Custodial provision for the young adult offender 1906–1974* (Dublin: Institute of Public Administration, 1975), p. 23.

57. See Desmond Bell, *Acts of Union: Youth culture and sectarianism in Northern Ireland* (London: Palgrave Macmillan, 1990); Stan Cohen, *Folk Devils and Moral Panics: The creation of the mods and rockers*, 3rd edn (London: Routledge, 2002); and David Fowler, *Youth Culture in Modern Britain, c.1920–c.1970* (Basingstoke: Palgrave, 2008).

58. Seán McConville, *Irish Political Prisoners 1920–1962: Pilgrimage of desolation* (Abingdon: Routledge, 2014), p. 835.

59. Anna Bryson, Kieran McEvoy and Allely Albert, 'Political Prisoners and the Conflict 100 Years On', *Howard Journal of Crime and Justice*, vol. 60, no. 1, 2021, p. 82. By comparison, the Irish Republic's imprisonment rate for 1969 was twenty-two per 100,000 population (although this was bolstered by an enormous apparatus of 'coercive confinement' outside of the formal criminal justice system), while the rate for England and Wales was sixty-two per 100,000 population. See Mary Rogan, *Prison Policy in Ireland: Politics, penal-welfarism and political imprisonment* (London: Routledge, 2011); Eoin O'Sullivan and Ian O'Donnell, *Coercive Confinement in Ireland: Patients, prisoners and penitents* (Manchester: Manchester University Press, 2012); and Grahame Allen and Noel Dempsey, *Prison Population Statistics* (Briefing Paper No. SN/SG/04334, House of Commons Library, London, 2016).

60. Mike Tomlinson, 'Imprisoned Ireland', in Vincenzo Ruggiero, Mike Ryan and Joe Sim (eds), *Western European Penal Systems* (Sage: London, 1995), p. 201.

61. David O'Mahony and Tim Chapman, 'Probation, the State and Community: Delivering probation services in Northern Ireland,' in Loraine Gelsthorpe and Rod Morgan (eds), *Handbook of Probation* (Cullompton: Willan, 2007), p. 158.

62. Nial Osborough, 'Probation in Northern Ireland', *Irish Jurist*, vol. 9, no. 2, 1974, p. 251.

63. Ibid.

64. Nicola Carr, 'Probation and Community Sanctions', in Anne-Marie McAlinden and Claire Dwyer (eds), *Criminal Justice in Transition* (Oxford: Hart, 2016), p. 232.

65. Laura Donohue, 'Regulating Northern Ireland: The Special Powers Acts, 1922–1972', *The Historical Journal*, vol. 41, no. 4, 1998, p. 1090.

66. Gerard Hogan and Clive Walker, *Political Violence and the Law in Ireland* (Manchester: Manchester University Press, 1989).

67. Whyte, 'How Much Discrimination?'

68. Donohue, 'Regulating Northern Ireland', p. 1090.

69. John McGarry and Brendan O'Leary, *Policing Northern Ireland* (Belfast: Blackstaff, 1999), p. 29.

70. Cited in Keith Jeffery, 'Police and Government in Northern Ireland', in Mark Mazower (ed.), *The Policing of Politics in the Twentieth Century* (Oxford: Berghahn, 1997), p. 161.

71. McGarry and O'Leary, *Policing Northern Ireland*, p. 29.

72. Ibid., p. 127.

73. John Hermon, *Holding the Line: An autobiography* (Dublin: Gill & Macmillan, 1997), pp. 13–15.

74. Chris Ryder, *The RUC, 1922–1997* (Oxford: Mandarin, 1997), p. 85.

75. Harris, *Prejudice and Tolerance in Ulster*, p. 131.

76. Alvin Jackson, *Ireland 1798–1998: War, peace and beyond*, 2nd edn (Chichester: Wiley, 2010), p. 335.

77. McGarry and O'Leary, *Policing Northern Ireland*, p. 31.

78. Whyte, 'How Much Discrimination?', p. 29.

79. Weitzer, *Policing Under Fire*.

80. Eamonn McCann, *War and an Irish Town*, 2nd edn (London: Pluto, 2010), pp. 10–11.

81. Former RUC officer, quoted in Ellison and Smyth, *The Crowned Harp*, p. 45.

82. Weitzer, *Policing Under Fire*, p. 51.

83. See generally, James Windle et al. (eds), *Criminology, Crime and Justice in Ireland* (London: Routledge, 2022); Tim Newburn, *Criminology*, 3rd edn (London: Routledge, 2017).

84. See, for example, Bew et al., *Northern Ireland 1921–2001*; O'Leary and McGarry, *Understanding Northern Ireland*; and Ruane and Todd, *The Dynamics of Conflict in Northern Ireland*.

85. John Brewer, Bill Lockhart and Paula Rodgers, *Crime in Ireland 1945–1995: Here be Dragons* (Oxford: Oxford University Press, 1997).

86. Historical Institutional Abuse Inquiry, *Report of the Historical Institutional Abuse Inquiry* (10 Volumes) (Belfast: Stationery Office, 2017).

87. In the Irish Republic, successive inquiries exposed the abusive regimes that many people in 'welfare' institutions endured. See O'Sullivan and O'Donnell, *Coercive Confinement in Ireland*.

88. See, generally, Niall Ó Dochartaigh, *From Civil Rights to Armalites: Derry and the birth of the Irish Troubles*, expanded 2nd edn (Basingstoke: Palgrave Macmillan, 2005); Lorenzo Bosi, 'The Dynamics of Social Movement Development: Northern Ireland's civil rights movement in the 1960s', *Mobilization*, vol. 11, no. 1, 2006, pp. 81–100; Simon Prince, *Northern Ireland's '68: Civil rights, global revolt and the origins of the Troubles*, revised edn (Dublin: Irish Academic Press, 2018); and Bob Purdie, *Politics in the Streets: The origins of the civil rights movement in Northern Ireland* (Belfast: Blackstaff Press, 1990).

89. David McKittrick, Seamus Kelters, Brian Feeney, Chris Thornton and David McVea, *Lost Lives: The stories of the men and women who died as a result of the Northern Ireland Troubles*, revised edn (London: Mainstream, 2007).

90. Scarman Tribunal, *Violence and Civil Disturbances in Northern Ireland in 1969*, p. 14.

91. Cameron Commission, *Disturbances in Northern Ireland: Report of the commission appointed by the governor of Northern Ireland*, Cmd 532 (Belfast: Stationery Office, 1969), pp. 72–4.

92. Scarman Tribunal, *Violence and Civil Disturbances in Northern Ireland in 1969*, pp. 15–16.

93. Ibid., p. 15.

CHAPTER 2: CONFLICT: 1969–98

1. Malcolm Sutton, *An Index of Deaths from the Conflict in Ireland*, available at: http://www.cain.ulst.ac.uk/sutton/.

2. Martin Melaugh, *Draft List of Deaths Related to the Conflict from 2002 to the Present* (2022), available at: http://cain.ulst.ac.uk/issues/violence/deathsfrom2002draft.htm.

3. David McKittrick, Seamus Kelters, Brian Feeney, Chris Thornton and David McVea, *Lost Lives: The stories of the men and women who died as a result of the Northern Ireland Troubles*, revised edn (London: Mainstream, 2007).

4. Sutton (*An Index of Deaths*) includes 116 deaths in the Republic of Ireland, 125 in Britain, and 18 in Europe, while McKittrick et al. (*Lost Lives*, p. 1559) include 125 in the Republic of Ireland, 128 in Britain, and 18 in Europe.

5. Richard Rose, *Northern Ireland: A time of choice* (Basingstoke: Macmillan, 1976), p. 26.

6. Bernadette Hayes and Ian McAllister, 'Sowing Dragon's Teeth: Public support for political violence and paramilitarism in Northern Ireland', *Political Studies* vol. 49, no. 5, 2001, p. 901.

7. Bernadette Hayes and Ian McAllister, 'Public Support for Political Violence and Paramilitarism in Northern Ireland and the Republic of Ireland', *Terrorism and Political Violence*, vol. 17, no. 4, 2005, pp. 600–1.

8. In other societies, high homicide rates are also evident, whether arising from armed conflicts, or other contexts such as violence related to organised crime. For wider discussion of various dimensions of organised violence in war settings, see Siniša Malešević, *The Sociology of War and Violence* (Cambridge: Cambridge University Press, 2010).

9. Rose, *Northern Ireland*, pp. 24–5.

10. Joe Ruane and Jennifer Todd, *The Dynamics of Conflict in Northern Ireland: Power, conflict and emancipation* (Cambridge: Cambridge University Press, 1996), p. 1; note that in some areas this rose to 80 per cent of the population.

11. Hayes and McAllister, 'Sowing Dragon's Teeth', p. 909.

12. Marie-Therese Fay, Mike Morrissey and Marie Smyth, *Northern Ireland's Troubles: The human costs* (London: Pluto, 1999).

13. McKittrick et al., *Lost Lives*, p. 1559.

14. Ian Gregory, Niall Cunningham, C. Lloyd, Ian Shuttleworth and Paul Ell, *Troubled Geographies: A spatial history of religion and society in Ireland* (Bloomington: Indiana University Press, 2013), p. 214.

15. John Darby, *Intimidation and the Control of Conflict in Northern Ireland* (Dublin: Gill & Macmillan, 1986).

16. Scarman Tribunal, *Violence and Civil Disturbances in Northern Ireland in 1969: Report of tribunal of inquiry*, Cmd 566 (Belfast: Stationery Office, 1972).

17. James Anderson and Ian Shuttleworth, 'Sectarian Demography, Territoriality and Political Development in Northern Ireland', *Political Geography*, vol. 17, no. 2, 1998, p. 189.

18. Neil Jarman, 'From War to Peace? Changing patterns of violence in Northern Ireland, 1990–2003', *Terrorism and Political Violence*, vol. 16, no. 3, 2004, pp. 420–38; Gregory et al., *Troubled Geographies*; Niall Cunningham and Ian Gregory, 'Hard to Miss, Easy to Blame? Peacelines, interfaces and political deaths in Belfast during the Troubles', *Political Geography*, vol. 40, May 2014, pp. 64–78.

19. Ruane and Todd, *The Dynamics of Conflict in Northern Ireland*, p. 1.

20. For valuable analyses of paramilitary organisations and their activities, see Steve Bruce, *The Red Hand: Protestant paramilitaries in Northern Ireland* (Oxford: Oxford University Press, 1992); Richard English, *Armed Struggle: The history of the IRA* (London: Pan, 2005); Ed Moloney, *A Secret History of the IRA* (London: Penguin, 2003); Niall Ó Dochartaigh, *Deniable Contact: Back-channel negotiation in Northern Ireland* (Oxford: Oxford University Press, 2021); Peter Taylor, *Provos: The IRA and Sinn Féin* (London: Bloomsbury, 1998), and *Loyalists* (London: Bloomsbury, 2000).

21. Sydney Elliott and William Flackes, *Northern Ireland: A political directory, 1968–1999* (Belfast: Blackstaff Press, 1999), pp. 685, 687.

22. Nicola Carr, 'The Criminal Justice System in Northern Ireland', in Steve Case, Phil Johnson, David Manlow, Roger Smith and Kate Williams (eds), *Criminology* (Oxford: Oxford University Press, 2017); and Kieran McEvoy, *Paramilitary Imprisonment in Northern Ireland* (Oxford: Oxford University Press, 2001).

23. McEvoy, *Paramilitary Imprisonment in Northern Ireland*, p. 16.

24. Mike Tomlinson, 'Imprisoned Ireland', in Vincenzo Ruggiero, Mike Ryan and Joe Sim (eds), *Western European Penal Systems* (Sage: London, 1995), p. 201.

25. McEvoy, *Paramilitary Imprisonment in Northern Ireland*, p. 225.

26. Quoted in David Beresford, *Ten Men Dead: The story of the 1981 Irish hunger strike* (London: Harper Collins, 1987), p. 44.

27. McEvoy, *Paramilitary Imprisonment in Northern Ireland*, p. 113.

28. Jim Campbell, Joe Duffy, Carol Tosone and David Falls, '"Just Get on with It": A qualitative study of social workers' experiences during the political conflict in Northern Ireland', *British Journal of Social Work*, vol. 51, no. 4, 2021, pp. 1314–31; Nicola Carr and Shadd Maruna, 'Legitimacy through Neutrality: Probation and the conflict in Northern Ireland', *Howard Journal of Criminal Justice*, vol. 51, no. 5, 2012, pp. 474–87.

29. Carr and Maruna, 'Legitimacy through Neutrality', p. 485.

30. Peter Shirlow and Kieran McEvoy, *Beyond the Wire: Former prisoners and conflict transformation in Northern Ireland* (London: Pluto Press, 2008), p. 2; Anna Bryson, Kieran McEvoy and Allely Albert, 'Political Prisoners and the Conflict, 100 Years On', *Howard Journal of Crime and Justice*, vol. 60, no. 1, 2021, pp. 79–91.

31. Consultative Group on the Past, *Report of the Consultative Group on the Past* (Belfast: Stationery Office, 2009), p. 64.

32. Cited in Bryson et al., 'Political Prisoners and the Conflict', p. 82.

33. Kieran McEvoy, David O'Mahony, Carol Horner and Olwen Lyner, 'The Home Front: The families of politically motivated

prisoners in Northern Ireland', *British Journal of Criminology*, vol. 39, no. 2, 1999, p. 178.

34. In 2001, an inquest found that the Ballymurphy victims were unarmed innocent civilians who posed no threat to soldiers ('Ballymurphy Massacre Victims "Innocent, Posed No Threat and Unconnected to Paramilitaries", Coroner Finds', *Belfast Telegraph*, 11 May 2021). In 2010 the Saville Report into Bloody Sunday found that the victims were innocent and the British prime minister called the killings 'unjustified and unjustifiable' ('Bloody Sunday Report: David Cameron Apologises for "Unjustifiable" Shootings', *Guardian*, 15 June 2010).

35. Kevin Boyle, Tom Hadden and Paddy Hillyard, *Law and State: The case of Northern Ireland* (London: Martin Robertson, 1975); Kevin Boyle, Tom Hadden and Paddy Hillyard, *Ten Years On: The legal control of political violence* (London: Cobden Trust, 1980); Hillyard, 'The Normalisation of Special Powers'; John Jackson and Sean Doran, *Judge Without Jury: Diplock trials in the adversary system* (Oxford: Clarendon, 1995); Fionnuala Ní Aoláin, *The Politics of Force: Conflict management and state violence in Northern Ireland* (Belfast: Blackstaff Press, 2000); Dermot Walsh, *The Use and Abuse of Emergency Legislation in Northern Ireland* (London: Cobden Trust, 1983).

36. Steven Greer and Anthony White, *Abolishing the Diplock Courts* (London: Cobden Trust, 1986), p. 78.

37. Boyle et al., *Law and State*, p. 148.

38. Jackson and Doran, *Judge Without Jury*.

39. Kieran McEvoy and Alex Schwartz, 'Judges, Conflict, and the Past', *Journal of Law and Society*, vol. 42, no. 4, 2015, p. 530.

40. Ibid.

41. The size of the RUC increased from approximately 3,000 officers in 1969 to over 11,000 officers by 1985. In addition to the regular force, an RUC Reserve force was also established of full-time and part-time personnel. The number of British Army personnel increased from 2,700 in 1969 to a peak of 30,300 in 1972 (including

8,500 members of the locally recruited Ulster Defence Regiment), declining to approximately 16,200 by 1985. Source: CAIN and PSNI.

42. Beresford, *Ten Men Dead*, p. 22.

43. Gardiner Committee, *Report of a Committee to Consider, in the Context of Civil Liberties and Human Rights, Measures to Deal with Terrorism in Northern Ireland* (London: Stationery Office, 1975), pp. 33–4.

44. Peter Taylor, *Beating the Terrorists? Interrogation at Armagh, Gough and Castlereagh* (London: Penguin, 1980).

45. McEvoy, *Paramilitary Imprisonment in Northern Ireland*; Mary Corcoran, *Out of Order: The political imprisonment of women in Northern Ireland 1972–1998* (Cullompton: Willan, 2006); Colin Crawford, *Defenders or Criminals? Loyalist prisoners and criminalisation* (Belfast: Blackstaff, 1999); Ruth Jamieson, 'Through the Lens of War: Political imprisonment in Northern Ireland', in Sandra Walklate and Ross McGarry (eds), *Criminology and War: Transgressing the borders* (London: Routledge, 2015). See also the website https://www.prisonsmemoryarchive.com for personal accounts from individuals involved with the prison system in some capacity during the conflict.

46. Ó Dochartaigh, *From Civil Rights to Armalites*.

47. The Anglo-Irish Agreement (AIA) was intended to bolster support for the SDLP and 'constitutional nationalism' in the face of the political advances being made by Sinn Féin following its decision to contest parliamentary elections in the early 1980s. For an assessment of the AIA and its long-term impact, see Arthur Aughey and Cathy Gormley-Heenan (eds), *The Anglo-Irish Agreement: Re-thinking its legacy* (Manchester: Manchester University Press, 2011).

48. For an assessment, see Ed Cairns, *Caught in the Crossfire: Children and the Northern Ireland conflict* (Belfast: Appletree Press, 1987); Caul, *The Juvenile Justice System in Northern Ireland*; Ken Heskin, 'Societal Disintegration in Northern Ireland: Fact or fiction?' *Economic and Social Review*, vol. 12, no. 2, 1981, pp. 93–113; and Kieran McEvoy, Brian Gormally and Harry Mika, 'Conflict, Crime Control, and the (re)Construction of State/Community Relations in

Northern Ireland', in Gordon Hughes, Eugene McLaughlin and John Muncie (eds), *Crime Prevention and Community Safety* (London: Sage, 2002).

49. The most recent updates are available on the PSNI website: https://www.psni.police.uk/about-us/our-publications-and-reports/official-statistics.

50. John Brewer, Bill Lockhart and Paula Rodgers, *Crime in Ireland 1945–1995: Here be Dragons* (Oxford: Oxford University Press, 1997), p. 37.

51. John Morison and Ray Geary, 'Crime, Conflict and Counting: Another commentary on Northern Ireland crime statistics', *Howard Journal of Criminal Justice*, vol. 28, no. 1, 1989, pp. 9–26; Robert Spjut, 'Criminal Statistics and Statistics on Security in Northern Ireland', *British Journal of Criminology*, vol. 23, no. 4, 1983, pp. 358–80.

52. Jan van Dijk and Patricia Mayhew, *Criminal Victimisation in the Industrialised World: Key findings of the 1989 and 1992 International Crime Surveys* (The Hague, Netherlands: Ministry of Justice, 1993), p. 34.

53. Pat Mayhew and Jan van Dijk, *Crime Victimisation in Eleven Industrialised Countries: Key findings from the 1996 International Crime Victims Survey* (Netherlands: WODC, 1997), p. 44.

54. Ibid, p. 66.

55. Michael Boyle and Tom Haire, *Fear of Crime and Likelihood of Victimisation in Northern Ireland* (Research Findings 2/96) (Belfast: Northern Ireland Office, 1996).

56. Northern Ireland Office, *'The Day of the Men and Women of Peace Must Surely Come …'* (Belfast: Northern Ireland Office, 1989), p. 37.

57. Police Authority of Northern Ireland, *Working Together to Police Northern Ireland* (Belfast: Police Authority of Northern Ireland, 1988), p. 2.

58. McEvoy et al. 'Conflict, Crime Control', pp. 185–6.

59. Mike Brogden, 'Burning Churches and Victim Surveys: The myth of Northern Ireland as a low-crime society', *Irish Journal of Sociology*, vol. 10, no. 1, 2000, pp. 27–48.

60. O'Mahony et al., *Crime, Community and Locale*.

61. Sandra Walklate (ed.), *Handbook of Victims and Victimology* (Abingdon: Routledge, 2012).

62. Fay et al., *Northern Ireland's Troubles*; Gregory et al., *Troubled Geographies*.

63. This discussion draws on arguments made in Mulcahy, *Policing Northern Ireland*. For a fuller discussion of these issues, see also Ellison and Smyth, *The Crowned Harp*, and Weitzer, *Policing Under Fire*.

64. John Brewer with Kathleen Magee, *Inside the RUC: Routine policing in a divided society* (Oxford: Clarendon, 1991).

65. Over the period 1970–98, a total of 359,699 house searches were carried out. Elliott and Flackes, *Northern Ireland*, p. 686. For further details of the census, see: https://www.nisra.gov.uk/publications/1971-census-reports.

66. Andrew Hamilton, Linda Moore and Tim Trimble, *Policing a Divided Society: Issues and perceptions in Northern Ireland* (Coleraine: University of Ulster, 1995), p. 62.

67. Robbie McVeigh, *'It's Part of Life Here ...': The security forces and harassment in Northern Ireland* (Belfast: Committee on the Administration of Justice, 1994), p. 101.

68. Whyte, *Interpreting Northern Ireland*, p. 87.

69. Ibid., p. 88.

70. Sutton, *An Index of Deaths*; Chris Ryder, *The RUC 1922–2000: A force under fire* (London: Arrow, 2000), p. 498.

71. Cited in Ryder, *The RUC 1922–2000*, p. 2.

72. Brewer and Magee, *Inside the RUC*, p. 115.

73. Helsinki Watch, *Children in Northern Ireland: Abused by security forces and paramilitaries* (New York: Human Rights Watch, 1992), p. 34; see also Brewer et al., 'Informal Social Control'.

74. Monica McWilliams, 'Masculinity and Violence: A gender perspective on crime in Northern Ireland', in Liam Kennedy (ed.), *Crime and Punishment in West Belfast* (Belfast: West Belfast Summer School, 1995).

75. Quoted in Mulcahy, *Policing Northern Ireland*, p. 77.

76. John Stalker, *Stalker* (London: Harrap, 1988).

77. Peter Taylor, *Brits: The war against the IRA* (London: Bloomsbury, 2001), pp. 248–9.

78. Quoted in Mulcahy, *Policing Northern Ireland*, p. 78.

79. Frank Kitson, *Low-Intensity Operations: Subversion, insurgency and peacekeeping*, 2nd edn (London: Faber & Faber, 1989).

80. Robin Evelegh, *Peace-Keeping in a Democratic Society: Lessons from Northern Ireland* (London: Hurst, 1978), p. 151.

81. Taylor, *Beating the Terrorists?*

82. Steven Greer, *Supergrasses: A study in anti-terrorist law enforcement in Northern Ireland* (Oxford: Oxford University Press, 1995), p. 57.

83. Sutton, *An Index of Deaths*.

84. Ron Dudai, 'Informers and the Transition in Northern Ireland', *British Journal of Criminology*, vol. 52, no. 1, 2012, pp. 32–54; Ron Dudai, 'Underground Penality: The IRA's punishment of informers', *Punishment and Society*, vol. 20, no. 3, 2018, pp. 375–95; Eleanor Leah Williams and Thomas Leahy, 'The "Unforgivable"? Irish Republican Army (IRA) informers and dealing with Northern Ireland conflict legacy, 1969–2021', *Intelligence and National Security*, vol. 38, no. 3, 2023, pp. 470–90.

85. *Belfast Telegraph*, 20 April 2012.

86. BBC News, 14 October 2016, 'Stakeknife: Investigation may result in prosecutions, John Boutcher says'. The investigation's report is due for release in 2023.

87. See, for example, https://www.irishtimes.com/obituaries/2023/04/15/freddie-scappaticci-obituary-ira-informer-stakeknife-was-known-as-jewel-in-the-crown-of-british-intelligence.

88. See, for example, 'Sinn Féin Man Admits He Was Agent', *BBC*, 16 December 2005. Donaldson was murdered at an isolated cottage in Donegal in 2006.

89. Thomas Leahy, *The Intelligence War Against the IRA* (Cambridge: Cambridge University Press, 2020).

90. Quoted in Mulcahy, *Policing Northern Ireland*, p. 80.

91. Independent Commission on Policing (ICP), *A New Beginning: Policing in Northern Ireland. Report of the Independent Commission on Policing for Northern Ireland* (Belfast: Stationery Office, 1999), p. 72.

92. See, generally, British Irish Rights Watch, *Deadly Intelligence: State involvement in loyalist murder in Northern Ireland* (London: British Irish Rights Watch, 1999); Anne Cadwallader, *Lethal Allies: British collusion in Ireland* (Cork: Mercier Press, 2013); Paddy Hillyard, 'Perfidious Albion: Collusion and cover-up in Northern Ireland', *Statewatch*, vol. 22, no. 4, 2013, pp. 1–14; Mark McGovern, *Counterinsurgency and Collusion in Northern Ireland* (London: Pluto, 2019); Raymond Murray, *State Violence in Northern Ireland, 1969–1997* (Cork: Mercier Press, 1998); Maurice Punch, *State Violence, Collusion and the Troubles: Counterinsurgency, government deviance and Northern Ireland* (London: Pluto, 2012); Bill Rolston, *Unfinished Business: State killings and the quest for truth* (Belfast: Beyond the Pale, 2000).

93. John Stevens, *Stevens Enquiry 3: Overview and recommendations* (London: Stationery Office, 2003), available at: https://cain.ulster.ac.uk/issues/collusion/chron.htm.

94. Office of the Police Ombudsman of Northern Ireland, *Operation Ballast: Investigation into the circumstances surrounding the murder of Raymond McCord Jr.* (Belfast: OPONI, 2007), p. 143.

95. Ibid., p. 144.

96. Moloney, *A Secret History of the IRA*; Mulcahy, *Policing Northern Ireland*, pp. 73–4; Relatives for Justice, *Collusion* (Derry: Relatives for Justice, 1995).

97. Spotlight, *Spotlight on the Troubles: A secret history*. Seven-part television series (2019), available at: youtube.com.

98. See, generally, Niamh Hourigan, John Morrison, James Windle and Andrew Silke, 'Crime in Ireland North and South: Feuding gangs and profiteering paramilitaries', *Trends in Organised Crime*, vol. 21, no. 1, 2018, pp. 126–46; John Jupp and Matthew Garrod, 'Legacies of the Troubles: The links between organized crime and terrorism in Northern Ireland', *Studies in Conflict & Terrorism*, vol. 45, nos. 5–6, 2022, pp. 389–428; Jon Moran, *Policing the Peace in Northern Ireland: Politics, crime and security after the Belfast Agreement* (Manchester: Manchester University Press, 2006).

99. Paddy Doherty, *Paddy Bogside* (Cork: Mercier Press, 2001), pp. 201–3, 183–5.

100. Paddy Hillyard, 'Popular Justice in Northern Ireland: Continuity and change', in Stephen Spitzer and Andrew Scull (eds), *Research on Law, Deviance and Social Control*, vol. 7 (Greenwich, CT: JAI Press, 1985); Jim McCorry and Mike Morrissey, 'Community, Crime and Punishment in West Belfast', *Howard Journal of Criminal Justice*, vol. 28, no. 4, 1989, pp. 282–90; Morrissey and Pease, 'The Importance of Northern Ireland'; Ronnie Munck, 'The Lads and the Hoods: Alternative justice in an Irish context', in Mike Tomlinson, Tony Varley and Ciaran McCullagh (eds), *Whose Law and Order?* (Belfast: Sociological Association of Ireland, 1988).

101. Colin Knox, '"See No Evil, Hear No Evil": Insidious paramilitary violence in Northern Ireland', *British Journal of Criminology*, vol. 42, no. 1, 2002, pp. 164–85; Rachel Monaghan, 'The Return of "Captain Moonlight": Informal justice in Northern Ireland', *Studies in Conflict and Terrorism*, vol. 25, no. 1, 2002, pp. 41–56; Jade Moran, 'Informal Justice in West Belfast: The local governance of anti-social behaviour in republican communities', unpublished PhD thesis, University of Cambridge, 2010; John Topping and Jonny Byrne, 'Paramilitary Punishments in Belfast: Policing beneath the peace', *Behavioral Sciences of Terrorism and Political Aggression*, vol. 4, no. 1, 2012, pp. 41–59.

102. The cover image of this book depicts a man tarred and feathered for 'theft' in the nationalist Bogside area of Derry in 1971. Although this form of punishment became less frequent in

later years, it nevertheless continued to occur sporadically. In 2007 a man was tarred and feathered in a loyalist area of Belfast, with a placard placed around his neck stating 'I'm a drug dealing scumbag'. See https://www.irishtimes.com/news/man-tarred-and-feathered-in-belfast-1.811373.

103. Quoted in Liam Kennedy, 'Nightmares within Nightmares: Paramilitary repression within working-class communities', in Liam Kennedy (ed.), *Crime and Punishment in West Belfast* (Belfast: West Belfast Summer School, 1995), p. 79. The full scale of expulsions is unclear, but one organisation providing support to victims recorded 453 expulsions – from specific towns, regions or Northern Ireland entirely – over the three-year period 1994–6. See Andrew Silke, 'The Lords of Discipline: The methods and motives of paramilitary vigilantism in Northern Ireland', *Low Intensity Conflict and Law Enforcement*, vol. 7, no. 2, 1998, p. 131.

104. Brewer et al., 'Informal Social Control'; Kennedy, *Crime and Punishment in West Belfast*; Northern Ireland Affairs Committee, *Composition, Recruitment and Training of the RUC*, HC 337 (London: Stationery Office, 1998).

105. Jonny Byrne and Lisa Monaghan, *Policing Republican and Loyalist Communities: Understanding key issues for local communities and the PSNI* (Belfast: Institute for Conflict Research, 2008); Weitzer, *Policing Under Fire*.

106. Mulcahy, *Policing Northern Ireland*, p. 36.

107. Bruce, *The Red Hand*, p. 198; Helsinki Watch, *Children in Northern Ireland*, pp. 43–4; Monaghan, 'The Return of "Captain Moonlight"'; Andrew Silke and Max Taylor, 'War without End: Comparing IRA and loyalist vigilantism in Northern Ireland', *Howard Journal of Criminal Justice*, vol. 39, no. 3, 2000, pp. 249–66; Tom Winston, 'Alternatives to Punishment Beatings and Shootings in a Loyalist Community in Belfast', *Critical Criminology*, vol. 8, no. 1, 1997, pp. 122–8.

108. Bruce, *The Red Hand*, p. 268.

109. Uğur Üngör, *Paramilitarism: Mass violence in the shadow of the state* (Oxford: Oxford University Press, 2020).

110. Hamill, *The Hoods*; Moran, 'Informal Justice'; Morrissey and Pease, 'The Importance of Northern Ireland'; Munck, 'The Lads and the Hoods'.

111. McCullough et al., *Car Theft in Northern Ireland*.

112. O'Mahony et al., *Crime, Community and Locale*, p. 50.

113. Sean O'Connell, 'From Toad of Toad Hall to the "Death Drivers" of Belfast: An exploratory history of "joyriding"', *British Journal of Criminology*, vol. 46, no. 3, 2006, pp. 455–69.

114. McCullough et al., *Car Theft in Northern Ireland*, p. 11.

115. Hamill, *The Hoods*, p. 146.

116. Sean O'Connell, 'Emotional Journeys: Belfast and the oral history of joyriding', *Oral History*, vol. 51, no. 1, 2023, pp. 59–69.

117. Karen McElrath, 'Drug Use and Drug Markets in the Context of Political Conflict: The case of Northern Ireland', *Addiction: Research and theory*, vol. 12, no. 6, 2004, pp. 577–90. For an analysis of related issues in Dublin, see Don Bennett, 'Are They Always Right? Investigation and proof in a citizen anti-heroin movement', in Mike Tomlinson, Tony Varley and Ciaran McCullagh (eds), *Whose Law and Order?* (Belfast: Sociological Association of Ireland, 1988).

118. Hamill, *The Hoods*.

119. Kennedy, *Crime and Punishment in West Belfast*; Knox, '"See No Evil, Hear No Evil"'.

120. *RUC Chief Constable's Annual Report for 1984* (Belfast: Stationery Office, 1985), p. xiii.

121. See, for example, Liam Kennedy, 'Nightmares Within Nightmares: Paramilitary repression within working-class communities', in Liam Kennedy (ed), *Crime and Punishment in West Belfast* (West Belfast Summer School, West Belfast, 1995).

122. Quoted in Mulcahy, *Policing Northern Ireland*, pp. 83–4.

123. O'Mahony et al., *Crime, Community and Locale*, p. 84. In Catholic lower-working-class urban communities, reporting rates to the police varied according to the seriousness of the crime.

Respondents were 'very likely' to report offences to the police in 43 per cent of cases of 'threats to harm or damage' and 85 per cent of cases where their home was broken into (p. 78).

124. Hayes and McAllister, 'Public Support', p. 607. It seems likely that the bulk of this support derives from wider political views on the legitimacy of the state, and with it, the legitimacy of violence to support or challenge it (Hayes and McAllister, 'Sowing Dragon's Teeth'). The higher levels of 'sympathy' for paramilitaries expressed by Catholics may reflect a greater willingness on their part to recognise a political motivation behind the activities of paramilitaries, both for republican and loyalist groups.

CHAPTER 3: TRANSITION: 1999–2022

1. See https://theconversation.com/belfast-has-more-peace-walls-now-than-25-years-ago-removing-them-will-be-a-complex-challenge-203975.

2. Mike Tomlinson, 'War, Peace and Suicide: The case of Northern Ireland', *International Sociology*, vol. 27, no. 4, 2012, pp. 464–82.

3. Comptroller and Auditor General, *Addiction Services in Northern Ireland* (Belfast: Northern Ireland Audit Office, 2020).

4. Brice Dickson, 'Criminal Justice Reform in Northern Ireland: The agents of change', in Anne-Marie McAlinden and Clare Dwyer (eds), *Criminal Justice in Transition: The Northern Ireland context* (Hart: Oxford, 2015), p. 67.

5. Phil Scraton, 'Prisons and Imprisonment in Northern Ireland', in Anne-Marie McAlinden and Clare Dwyer (eds), *Criminal Justice in Transition: The Northern Ireland context* (Hart: Oxford, 2015), p. 192. See also Michelle Butler, *The Northern Ireland Prison Reform Programme: Progress made and challenges remaining* (Knowledge Exchange Seminar Series Policy Briefing) (Belfast: Queen's University Belfast, 2018); and Azrini Wahidin, Linda Moore and Una Convery, 'Unlocking a Locked-down Regime: The role of penal policy and administration in Northern Ireland and the challenges of change', *The Howard Journal of Criminal Justice*, vol. 51, no 5, 2012, pp. 458–73.

6. Nicola Carr, 'Probation and Community Sanctions', in Anne-Marie McAlinden and Claire Dwyer (eds), *Criminal Justice in Transition* (Oxford: Hart, 2016).

7. John Jackson, 'Many Years On in Northern Ireland: The diplock legacy', *Northern Ireland Legal Quarterly*, vol. 60, no. 2, 2009, pp. 213–29; Dickson, 'Criminal Justice Reform in Northern Ireland'. In the Irish Republic, jury-less courts – 'Special Criminal Courts' – were established to deal primarily with political violence, including the threat of jury-tampering. However, more recently they have increasingly been used to deal with organised crime. See, generally, Aogán Mulcahy, 'The Impact of the Northern "Troubles" in Criminal Justice in the Irish Republic', in Paul O'Mahony (ed.), *Criminal Justice in Ireland* (Dublin: Institute for Public Administration, 2002).

8. Independent Commission on Policing (ICP), *A New Beginning: Policing in Northern Ireland. Report of the Independent Commission on Policing for Northern Ireland* (Belfast: Stationery Office, 1999), p. 2.

9. Clifford Shearing, '"A New Beginning" for Policing', *Journal of Law and Society*, vol. 27, no. 3, 2000, pp. 386–7.

10. *Irish Times*, 10 September 1999.

11. DUP press release, 9 September 1999. The 'ethnic cleansing' reference was to the ICP's recommendations for measures to increase Catholic recruitment by establishing a 50:50 (Catholic:non-Catholic) recruitment system (discussed further below).

12. See: http://news.bbc.co.uk/2/hi/uk_news/northern_ireland/455588.stm.

13. Aogán Mulcahy, *Policing Northern Ireland: Conflict, legitimacy and reform* (Cullompton: Willan, 2006).

14. Oversight Commissioner, *Overseeing the Proposed Revisions for the Policing Services of Northern Ireland – Report 19 (Final Report)* (Belfast: Office of the Oversight Commissioner, 2007), p. 8.

15. Graham Ellison, 'A Blueprint for Democratic Policing Anywhere in the World? Police reform, political transition, and conflict

resolution in Northern Ireland', *Police Quarterly*, vol. 10, no. 3, 2007, p. 243.

16. Chris Patten, 'Personal Reflections on Chairing the Commission', in David Doyle (ed.), *Policing the Narrow Ground: Lessons from the transformation of policing in Northern Ireland* (Dublin: Royal Irish Academy, 2010), p. 25.

17. Clifford Shearing, 'The Curious Case of the *Patten Report*', in David Doyle (ed.), *Policing the Narrow Ground: Lessons from the transformation of policing in Northern Ireland* (Dublin: Royal Irish Academy, 2010), p. 29.

18. Patten, 'Personal Reflections on Chairing the Commission', p. 25.

19. Aogán Mulcahy, 'Great Expectations and Complex Realities: The impact and implications of the police reform process in Northern Ireland', in Jennifer Brown (ed.), *The Future of Policing* (London: Routledge, 2014).

20. For further discussion on the relationship between community composition and attitudes to the police, see Ben Bradford, John Topping, Richard Martin and Jonathan Jackson, 'Can Diversity Promote Trust? Neighbourhood context and trust in the police in Northern Ireland', *Policing and Society*, vol. 29, no. 9, 2019, pp. 1022–41.

21. Northern Ireland Affairs Committee, *The Northern Ireland Prison Service*, HC 118 (London: Stationery Office, 2007).

22. Michael von Tangen Page, 'A "Most Difficult and Unpalatable Part": The release of politically motivated violent offenders', in Michael Cox, Adrian Guelke and Fiona Stephen (eds), *A Farewell to Arms? Beyond the Good Friday Agreement* (Manchester: Manchester University Press, 2006), p. 201.

23. Kieran McEvoy, *Amnesties, Prosecutions and the Rule of Law in Northern Ireland*, House of Commons Defence Select Committee Briefing Paper, 2017, p. 18; see also Clare Dwyer, 'Risk, Politics and the "Scientification" of Political Judgement: Prisoner release and conflict transformation in Northern Ireland', *British Journal of Criminology*, vol. 47, no. 5, 2007, pp. 779–97.

24. A study of criminal reconvictions (as opposed to re-imprisonment) in Northern Ireland found that 47 per cent of those released from prison were reconvicted within two years of release. See Department of Justice, *Adult Reconviction in Northern Ireland 2005*, Research and Statistical Bulletin 1/2011 (Belfast: Department of Justice, 2011). A major study of recidivism in the Republic of Ireland found that 49 per cent of those released from prison were reimprisoned within four years. See Ian O'Donnell, Eric Baumer and Nicola Hughes, 'Recidivism in the Republic of Ireland', *Criminology and Criminal Justice*, vol. 8, no. 2, 2008, pp. 123–46.

25. Anna Bryson, Kieran McEvoy and Allely Albert, 'Political Prisoners and the Irish Conflict 100 Year On', *Howard Journal*, vol. 60, no. 1, 2021, p. 88.

26. Department of Justice, *The Northern Ireland Prison Population 2021/22 (Revised)* (Belfast: Department of Justice, 2022), p. 20.

27. These replaced the previous system of police authorities which oversaw the local governance of policing for the different police services across Britain. For further details, see: https://www.apccs.police.uk/.

28. Her Majesty's Inspector of Constabulary, *Responding to Austerity: The Police Service of Northern Ireland* (London: Stationery Office, 2015).

29. See, for example, https://www.theguardian.com/uk-news/2017/jun/04/northern-ireland-police-cuts-mean-unsolved-troubles-cases-might-be-dropped.

30. Anne-Marie McAlinden and Clare Dwyer, '"Doing" Criminal Justice in Northern Ireland: "Policy transfer", transitional justice and governing through the past', in Anne-Marie McAlinden and Clare Dwyer (eds), *Criminal Justice in Transition: The Northern Ireland context* (Hart: Oxford, 2015), p. 374.

31. Ibid.

32. Peter Leary, *Unapproved Routes: Histories of the Irish border, 1922–1972* (Oxford: Oxford University Press, 2016). Border communities celebrated the nous and local knowledge that enabled

them to evade customs and police officers and thwart state authority. For the police, however, cross-border smuggling posed significant challenges. For example: 'In December 1951, seventy stick-wielding farmers surrounded a police Sergeant and Constable after they attempted to seize four bullocks at a fair' in Garrison, County Fermanagh (p. 154).

33. For wider discussion of Brexit's implications for Northern Ireland, see Chris Gilligan, 'Methodological Nationalism and the Northern Ireland Blind-Spot in Ethnic and Racial Studies', *Ethnic and Racial Studies*, vol. 45, no. 3, 2022, pp. 431–51; and Mary Murphy and Jonathan Evershed, 'Contesting Sovereignty and Borders: Northern Ireland, devolution and the union', *Territory, Politics, Governance*, vol. 10, no. 5, 2022, pp. 661–77.

34. Neil Jarman, 'From War to Peace? Changing patterns of violence in Northern Ireland, 1990–2003', *Terrorism and Political Violence*, vol. 16, no. 3, 2004, pp. 420–38; Roger Mac Ginty, *No War, No Peace: The rejuvenation of stalled peace processes and peace accords* (Basingstoke: Palgrave Macmillan, 2006); Christina Steenkamp, 'In the Shadows of War and Peace: Making sense of violence after peace accords', *Conflict, Security and Development*, vol. 11, no. 3, 2011, pp. 357–83.

35. ICP, *A New Beginning*, p. 76.

36. Jarman, 'From War to Peace?', p. 425.

37. Fred Vincent, *Everyone Got a Hug That Morning ...: From desecration to reconciliation* (Belfast: Institute for Conflict Research, 2009), p. 7.

38. Niamh Hourigan, John Morrison, James Windle and Andrew Silke, 'Crime in Ireland North and South: Feuding gangs and profiteering paramilitaries', *Trends in Organised Crime*, vol. 21, no. 1, 2018, pp. 126–46; John Jupp and Matthew Garrod, 'Legacies of the Troubles: The links between organized crime and terrorism in Northern Ireland', *Studies in Conflict & Terrorism*, vol. 45, nos. 5–6, 2022, pp. 389–428; Jon Moran, *Policing the Peace in Northern Ireland: Politics, crime and security after the Belfast Agreement* (Manchester: Manchester University Press, 2006).

39. Brian Hollywood, 'Dancing in the Dark: Ecstasy, the dance culture and moral panic in post-ceasefire Northern Ireland', *Critical Criminology*, vol. 8, no. 1, 2007, pp. 62–77; Karen McElrath, 'Drug Use and Drug Markets in the Context of Political Conflict: The case of Northern Ireland', *Addiction: Research and theory*, vol. 12, no. 6, 2004, pp. 577–90.

40. For example, in February 2023, a senior PSNI detective, John Caldwell, was shot and seriously injured by dissident republican paramilitaries (https://www.bbc.com/news/uk-northern-ireland-65711267).

41. Steenkamp, 'In the Shadows of War and Peace'.

42. See, generally, Brian Hanley, *Republicanism, Crime and Paramilitary Policing, 2016–2020* (Cork: Cork University Press, 2022).

43. See the 2021 BBC television documentary, *Heist: The Northern Bank robbery*, available at: https://www.youtube.com/watch?v=sLbYzMRU4GI.

44. Following widespread public criticism and political pressure, the IRA released a statement outlining its investigation into the events, including its offer to shoot those responsible. See 'Full Text of IRA Statement', *Guardian*, 8 May 2005.

45. Independent Monitoring Commission, *Seventh Report of the Independent Monitoring Commission* (HC 546) (London: Stationery Office, 2005), p. 33.

46. Northern Ireland Affairs Committee, *Organised Crime in Northern Ireland* (London: Stationery Office, 2006), p. 10.

47. Neil Jarman, *Criminal Justice Responses to Hate Crime in Northern Ireland* (Belfast: Institute for Conflict Research, 2012); Neil Jarman, 'Acknowledgement, Recognition and Response: The criminal justice system and hate crime in Northern Ireland', in Amanda Haynes, Jennifer Schweppe and Seamus Taylor (eds), *Critical Perspectives on Hate Crime* (London: Palgrave, 2017); Roger Mac Ginty, 'Hate Crimes in Deeply Divided Societies: The case of Northern Ireland', *New Political Science*, vol. 22, no. 1, 2000, pp. 49–60; Robbie McVeigh, 'Hate and the State: Northern Ireland,

sectarian violence and "perpetrator-less crime"', in Amanda Haynes, Jennifer Schweppe and Seamus Taylor (eds), *Critical Perspectives on Hate Crime* (London: Palgrave, 2017); Northern Ireland Affairs Committee, *The Challenge of Diversity: Hate crime in Northern Ireland* (HC 548-1) (London: Stationery Office, 2005).

48. Northern Ireland Policing Board, *Thematic Review of Policing Race Hate Crime* (Belfast: NIPB, 2017), pp. 96–7.

49. Police figures are updated on an ongoing basis, so for example the Statistical Bulletin for 2022/23 includes minor revisions for crime levels in previous years. As a result, figures for the same year can differ across publications. The most recent figures are used here, albeit recognising that figures for 2022/23 and other years may be amended in future police publications.

50. Note that because of the changes in how detections were classified, the detection rates vary across publications. The figures used here include the retrospective application of the most recent classification scheme. See Police Service of Northern Ireland, *Police Recorded Crime in Northern Ireland: Update to 31st March 2023* (Belfast: PSNI, 2023).

51. For instance, the drop in detection rate between 2000/1 and 2001/2 was largely attributed to the introduction of a new information management system that recorded a greater number of low-level offences which are less likely to be cleared up, while the drop between 2005/6 and 2006/7 was attributed to a higher evidential standard being introduced when the Public Prosecution Service was established. The drop in 2007/8 was attributed to the discontinuation of methods of claiming detections for some minor crimes. Further changes were introduced in 2010/11 and 2011/12 whereby 'discretionary disposals' and 'penalty notices for disorder' were included in the 'outcome' figures. See, generally, PSNI, *Police Recorded Crime Annual Trends 1998/99 to 2021/22* (Belfast: PSNI, 2022).

52. Ibid., p. 7; PSNI, *Police Recorded Crime in Northern Ireland: Update to 31st March 2023*, p. 6.

53. Criminal Justice Inspection Northern Ireland (CJINI), *Domestic Violence and Abuse: A follow-up review of inspection recommendations* (Belfast: CJINI, 2013).

54. See PSNI, *Police Recorded Crime Annual Trends 1998/99 to 2021/22*, section 9. After the 1994 paramilitary ceasefires, regional variations remained a significant feature of crime levels: 'The more violence a local area experiences, and the larger the proportion of this violence committed by anti-government groups, the more violent crime it sees in the aftermath of war.' See Annekatrin Deglow, 'Localized Legacies of Civil War: Postwar violent crime in Northern Ireland', *Journal of Peace Research*, vol. 53, no. 6, 2016, p. 796.

55. John van Kesteren, Pat Mayhew and Paul Nieuwbeerta, *Criminal Victimisation in Seventeen Industrialised Countries: Key findings from the 2000 International Crime Victims Survey* (The Hague: Ministry of Justice, 2000), p. 38.

56. Jan van Dijk, John van Kesteren and Paul Smit, *Criminal Victimisation in International Perspective: Key findings from the 2004–2005 ICVS and EU ICS* (The Hague: Ministry of Justice, 2007).

57. Ibid., p. 46.

58. Jan van Dijk, Andromachi Tseloni and Graham Farrell (eds), *The International Crime Drop* (Basingstoke: Palgrave Macmillan, 2012). There does seem to be evidence that Catholics in particular were more willing to report crime to the police than previously, but not to an extent that this could explain the rise in recorded crime. See Ipsos MORI, *Research into Recent Crime Trends in Northern Ireland* (Belfast: Ipsos MORI, 2007).

59. P. Campbell, A. Rice and K. Ross, *Experience of Crime: Findings from the 2019/20 Northern Ireland Safe Community Survey* (Belfast: Department of Justice, 2021).

60. Ibid., p. 7.

61. K. Ross and M. Beggs, *Experience of Crime and Perceptions of Crime and Policing and Justice: Findings from the 2021/22 Northern Ireland Safe Community Telephone Survey* (Belfast: Department of Justice, 2023), p. 6.

62. Graham Ellison and Mary O'Rawe, 'Security Governance in Transition: The compartmentalizing, crowding out and corralling of policing and security in Northern Ireland', *Theoretical Criminology*,

vol. 14, no. 1, 2010, pp. 31–57; Aogán Mulcahy, 'Community Policing in Contested Settings: The Patten Report and police reform in Northern Ireland', in Tom Williamson (ed.), *The Handbook of Knowledge-Based Policing* (Chichester: Wiley, 2008).

63. The word 'Boards' was omitted from their official title when they were established under subsequent legislation, presumably to indicate that their role was largely limited to consultation.

64. ICP, *A New Beginning*, p. 35.

65. Mulcahy, *Policing Northern Ireland*.

66. Ibid., p. 175.

67. Ellison and O'Rawe, 'Security Governance in Transition'.

68. CJINI, *Policing and Community Safety Partnerships: A review of governance, delivery and outcomes* (Belfast: CJINI, 2014).

69. See also the 2021 Life and Times Survey module on 'Community Safety' (https://www.ark.ac.uk/nilt/2021/Community_safety/).

70. Jonny Byrne and John Topping, *Community Safety: A decade of development, delivery, challenge and change in Northern Ireland* (Belfast: Belfast Conflict Resolution Consortium, 2012).

71. CJINI, *Community Restorative Justice Ireland: Report of an inspection* (Belfast: CJINI, 2008); CJINI, *Community Restorative Justice Ireland: A pre-accreditation inspection of north Belfast and south and east Belfast Community Restorative Justice Ireland schemes* (Belfast: CJINI, 2014). Further details of these initiatives are available at: https://www.crjireland.org/ and https://alternativesrj.co.uk/. For a wider discussion on the potential of restorative justice in different contexts, see Jonathan Doak and David O'Mahony, 'In Search of Legitimacy: Restorative youth conferencing in Northern Ireland', *Legal Studies*, vol. 31, no. 2, 2011, pp. 305–25; Anna Eriksson, *Justice in Transition: Community restorative justice in Northern Ireland* (Cullompton: Willan, 2009); and Colin Knox, 'From the Margins to the Mainstream: Community restorative justice in Northern Ireland', *Journal of Peacekeeping and Development*, vol. 8, no. 2, 2013, pp. 57–72.

72. *Irish Times*, 2 December 2004.

73. See: http://www.belfasttelegraph.co.uk/news/local-national/ northern-ireland/police-refused-to-chase-attackers-into-a-nogo-area-28759907.html.

74. John Topping, 'Accountability, Policing and the Police Service of Northern Ireland: Local practice, global standards?', in Stuart Lister and Michael Rowe (eds), *Accountability of Policing* (London: Routledge, 2016), p. 159.

75. Oversight Commissioner, *Overseeing the Proposed Revisions*, pp. 3, 212.

76. Graham Ellison, Pete Shirlow and Nathan Pino, 'Assessing the Determinants of Public Confidence in the Police: A case study of a post-conflict community in Northern Ireland', *Criminology and Criminal Justice*, vol. 13, no. 5, 2013, p. 564.

77. Ibid.; Graham Ellison, Pete Shirlow and Aogán Mulcahy, 'Responsible Participation, Community Engagement, and Policing in Transitional Societies: Lessons from a local crime survey in Northern Ireland', *Howard Journal of Criminal Justice*, vol. 51, no. 5, 2012, pp. 488–502.

78. Priscilla Hayner, *Unspeakable Truths: Transitional justice and the challenge of truth commissions*, 2nd edn (London: Routledge, 2010).

79. Lea David, *The Past Can't Heal Us: The dangers of mandating memory in the name of human rights* (Cambridge: Cambridge University Press, 2020).

80. John Brewer and Bernadette Hayes, 'Victimhood Status and Public Attitudes Towards Post-conflict Agreements: Northern Ireland as a case study', *Political Studies*, vol. 61, no. 2, 2013, pp. 442–61; Claire Hackett and Bill Rolston, 'The Burden of Memory: Victims, storytelling and resistance in Northern Ireland', *Memory Studies*, vol. 2, no. 3, 2009, pp. 355–76; Cheryl Lawther, *Truth, Denial and Transition: Northern Ireland and the contested past* (Abingdon: Routledge, 2014); Bill Rolston and Mairead Gilmartin, *Unfinished Business: State killings and the quest for truth* (Belfast: Beyond the Pale, 2000).

81. See https://www.govinfo.gov/content/pkg/CHRG-106hhrg64523/html/CHRG-106hhrg64523.htm.

82. ICP, *A New Beginning*, p. 3.

83. See George Hamilton, 'Chief Constable's Speech to "Victimhood and Dealing With the Past in Northern Ireland" Conference at Queen's University Belfast, 14 May 2018, available at: https://www.belfasttelegraph.co.uk/news/northern-ireland/full-text-chief-constable-george-hamiltons-speech/36909313.html; Paddy Hillyard, 'Perfidious Albion: Collusion and cover-up in Northern Ireland', *Statewatch*, vol. 22, no. 4, 2013, pp. 1–14; Mark McGovern, *Counterinsurgency and Collusion in Northern Ireland* (London: Pluto, 2019); Lawther, *Truth, Denial and Transition*; and Maurice Punch, *State Violence, Collusion and the Troubles: Counterinsurgency, government deviance and Northern Ireland* (London: Pluto, 2012).

84. Consultative Group on the Past, *Report of the Consultative Group on the Past* (Belfast: Stationery Office, 2009).

85. Patricia Lundy, 'Can the Past Be Policed? Lessons from the Historical Enquiries Team Northern Ireland', *Journal of Law and Social Challenges*, vol. 11, Spring–Summer, 2009, pp. 109–71; Patricia Lundy, 'Paradoxes and Challenges of Transitional Justice at the "Local" Level: Historical enquiries in Northern Ireland', *Contemporary Social Science*, vol. 6, no. 1, 2011, pp. 89–105; Sir Hugh Orde, 'Policing the Past to Police the Future', *International Review of Law, Computers and Technology*, vol. 20, nos. 1–2, 2006, pp. 37–48.

86. Oversight Commissioner, *Overseeing the Proposed Revisions*.

87. Her Majesty's Inspectorate of Constabulary, *Inspection of the Police Service of Northern Ireland Historical Enquiries Team* (London: Stationery Office, 2013), p. 100.

88. Office of the Police Ombudsman of Northern Ireland, *Operation Ballast*.

89. Criminal Justice Inspection Northern Ireland, *An Inspection into the Independence of the Office of the Police Ombudsman for Northern Ireland* (Belfast: CJINI, 2011).

90. For further details, see Patrick Keefe, *Say Nothing: A true story of murder and memory in Northern Ireland* (London: William Collins, 2018).

91. RTÉ, 30 July 2020 (https://www.rte.ie/news/2020/0730/1156503-troubles-court/).

92. RTÉ, 2 July 2021 (https://www.rte.ie/news/2021/0702/1232632-derry-bloody-sunday-prosecutions/); and 22 September 2022 (https://www.rte.ie/news/regional/2022/0922/1324883-soldier-f-pps/).

93. Criminal Justice Inspection Northern Ireland, *A Review of the Cost and Impact of Dealing with the Past on Criminal Justice Organisations in Northern Ireland* (Belfast: CJINI, 2013), p. 44.

94. Ibid., p. 6.

95. *Irish Times*, 6 June 2014, p. 9.

96. RTÉ, 14 July 2021 (https://www.rte.ie/news/2021/0714/1234949-british-troubles-amnesty/).

97. See, for example, Committee on the Administration of Justice (CAJ)/Queen's University Belfast, *Briefing from the Queen's University School of Law and CAJ Model Bill Team – Northern Ireland Troubles (Legacy and Reconciliation) Bill Second Reading, House of Lords, 23 November 2022* (Belfast: CAJ, 2022).

CONCLUSION

1. John Brewer, Bill Lockhart and Paula Rodgers, 'Informal Social Control and Crime Management in Belfast', *British Journal of Sociology*, vol. 49, no. 4, 1998, pp. 570–85; John Darby, *Intimidation and the Control of Conflict in Northern Ireland* (Dublin: Gill & Macmillan, 1986).

2. John Brewer, Bill Lockhart and Paula Rodgers, *Crime in Ireland 1945–1995: Here be Dragons* (Oxford: Oxford University Press, 1997), p. 220.

3. Ed Cairns, *Caught in the Crossfire: Children and the Northern Ireland conflict* (Belfast: Appletree Press, 1987), p. 93.

4. Siniša Malešević and Niall Ó Dochartaigh, 'Why Combatants Fight: The Irish Republican Army and the Bosnian Serb Army compared', *Theory and Society*, vol. 47, no. 3, 2018, pp. 293–326.

5. Jan van Dijk, Andromachi Tseloni and Graham Farrell (eds), *The International Crime Drop* (Basingstoke: Palgrave Macmillan, 2012).

6. See, generally, Gary LaFree and Andromachi Tseloni, 'Democracy and Crime: A multilevel analysis of homicide trends in forty-four countries, 1950–2000', *Annals of the American Academy of Political and Social Science*, vol. 605, no. 1, 2006, pp. 26–49; Christina Steenkamp, 'In the Shadows of War and Peace: Making sense of violence after peace accords', *Conflict, Security and Development*, vol. 11, no. 3, 2011, p. 378; and Roger Mac Ginty, *No War, No Peace: The rejuvenation of stalled peace processes and peace accords* (Basingstoke: Palgrave Macmillan, 2006).

7. See, for example, Northern Ireland Affairs Committee, *Organised Crime in Northern Ireland* (London: Stationery Office, 2006).

8. Victor Asal, R. Karl Rethemeyer and Eric W. Schoon, 'Crime, Conflict, and the Legitimacy Trade-Off: Explaining variation in insurgents' participation in crime', *Journal of Politics*, vol. 81, no. 2, 2019, pp. 399–410.

9. David O'Mahony, Ray Geary, Kieran McEvoy and John Morison, *Crime, Community and Locale: The Northern Ireland Communities Crime Survey* (Aldershot: Ashgate, 2000), p. 120; see also Brewer et al., *Crime in Ireland 1945–1995*, p. 222.

10. See, for example, Criminal Justice Inspection Northern Ireland, *Domestic Violence and Abuse: A follow-up review of inspection recommendations* (Belfast: CJINI, 2013); and Neil Jarman, 'Acknowledgement, Recognition and Response: The criminal justice system and hate crime in Northern Ireland', in Amanda Haynes, Jennifer Schweppe and Seamus Taylor (eds), *Critical Perspectives on Hate Crime* (London: Palgrave, 2017).

11. See, for example, Heather Hamill, *The Hoods: Crime and punishment in Belfast* (Princeton, NJ: Princeton University Press, 2011); Ken Harland, 'Violent Youth Culture in Northern Ireland: Young men, violence, and the challenges of peacebuilding', *Youth and Society*, vol. 43, no. 2, 2011, pp. 414–32; and Colm Walsh and Dirk Schubotz, 'Young Men's Experiences of Violence and Crime in a Society Emerging from Conflict', *Journal of Youth Studies*, vol. 23, no. 5, 2020, pp. 650–66.

12. Bernadette Hayes and Ian McAllister, 'Public Support for Political Violence and Paramilitarism in Northern Ireland and the Republic of Ireland', *Terrorism and Political Violence*, vol. 17, no. 4, 2005, pp. 599–617.

13. Ronald Weitzer, *Policing Under Fire: Ethnic conflict and police–community relations in Northern Ireland* (Albany: SUNY, 1995), p. 137.

14. Northern Ireland Affairs Committee, *Organised Crime in Northern Ireland* (London: Stationery Office, 2006).

15. The use of proxies is a well-established element of state deviance. See Ruth Jamieson and Kieran McEvoy, 'State Crime by Proxy and Juridical Othering', *British Journal of Criminology*, vol. 45, no. 4, 2005, pp. 504–27.

16. Paddy Hillyard and Steve Tombs, 'Social Harm and Zemiology', in Alison Liebling, Shadd Maruna and Lesley McAra (eds), *The Oxford Handbook of Criminology* (Oxford: Oxford University Press, 2017).

17. The post-9/11 wars in Iraq, Afghanistan, Yemen, Syria and Pakistan led to almost 390,000 civilian deaths in those countries by 2021, with more than 3.5 million others dying indirectly from these conflicts. See the 'Costs of War' project (https://watson.brown.edu/costsofwar/costs/human/civilians).

18. As one feature of this, the IRA adjusted its definition of 'legitimate targets' to enable it to pursue its objectives while also seeking to maintain a necessary level of support among the wider republican community and deflect criticism that specific activities generated. See John Darby, 'Legitimate Targets: A control on violence', in Adrian Guelke (ed.), *New Perspectives on the Northern Ireland Conflict* (Aldershot: Avebury, 1996).

19. Anne-Marie McAlinden and Clare Dwyer (eds), *Criminal Justice in Transition: The Northern Ireland context* (Oxford: Hart, 2015).

20. Graham Ellison, 'A Blueprint for Democratic Policing Anywhere in the World? Police reform, political transition, and conflict resolution in Northern Ireland', *Police Quarterly*, vol. 10, no. 3, 2007, pp. 243–69; Aogán Mulcahy, 'Community Policing in

Contested Settings: The Patten Report and police reform in Northern Ireland', in Tom Williamson (ed.), *The Handbook of Knowledge-Based Policing: Current conceptions and future directions* (Chichester: Wiley, 2008); Aogán Mulcahy, 'Great Expectations and Complex Realities: The impact and implications of the police reform process in Northern Ireland', in Jennifer Fleming (ed.), *The Future of Policing* (London: Routledge, 2013).

21. Graham Ellison and Conor O'Reilly, 'From Empire to Iraq and the "War on Terror": The transplantation and commodification of the (Northern) Irish policing experience', *Police Quarterly*, vol. 11, no. 4, 2008, pp. 395–426; and Graham Ellison and Conor O'Reilly, '"Ulster's Policing Goes Global": The police reform process in Northern Ireland and the creation of a global brand', *Crime, Law and Social Change*, vol. 50, nos. 4–5, 2008, pp. 331–51.

22. David Bayley, 'Post-Conflict Police Reform: Is Northern Ireland a model?', *Policing*, vol. 2, no. 2, 2008, p. 240.

23. Ibid.

24. Graham Ellison and Nathan Pino, *Globalisation, Development and Security Sector Reform* (London: Macmillan, 2012), p. 214.

25. For an analysis of how 'human rights' is mediated through the political complexion of the Policing Board and the wider environment, see Richard Martin, 'Ethno-national Narratives of Human Rights: The Northern Ireland Policing Board', *Modern Law Review*, vol. 83, no. 1, 2020, pp. 91–127.

26. See, generally, Trevor Jones and Tim Newburn, 'When Crime Policies Travel: Cross-national policy transfer in crime control', *Crime and Justice*, vol. 50, 2021, pp. 115–62.

27. Priscilla Hayner, *Unspeakable Truths: Transitional justice and the challenge of truth commissions*, 2nd edn (London: Routledge, 2010).

28. Ruti Teitel, *Transitional Justice* (Oxford: Oxford University Press, 2000).

29. Lea David, *The Past Can't Heal Us: The dangers of mandating memory in the name of human rights* (Cambridge: Cambridge University Press, 2020), pp. 1–2.

30. Ibid., p. 2.

31. David Smith and Gerry Chambers, *Inequality in Northern Ireland* (Oxford: Clarendon Press, 1991).

32. Richard Breen, 'Class Inequality and Social Mobility in Northern Ireland, 1973 to 1996', *American Sociological Review*, vol. 65, no. 3, 2000, pp. 392–406; Neil Rowland, Duncan McVicar and Ian Shuttleworth, 'The Evolution of Catholic/Protestant Unemployment Inequality in Northern Ireland, 1983–2016', *Population, Space and Place*, vol. 28, no. 4, 2022, pp. 1–16 (https://doi.org/10.1002/psp.2525).

33. Stephanie Burns, Ruth Leith and Joanne Hughes, *Education Inequalities in Northern Ireland* (Belfast: Equality Commission for Northern Ireland, 2015).

34. Peter Shirlow and Colin Coulter, 'Northern Ireland: 20 years after the cease-fires', *Studies in Conflict and Terrorism*, vol. 37, no. 9, 2014, p. 719.

35. The Belfast Agreement provides for a referendum to be held on the future of Northern Ireland. At this stage, surveys suggest that a referendum on the prospect of the unification of Ireland would be rejected, although demographic and political trends suggest that support for it is likely to increase in the coming years. In these circumstances, it seems inevitable that this issue will be a feature of the political landscape for the foreseeable future. See https://www.irishtimes.com/ireland/2022/12/03/poll-shows-northern-ireland-rejects-unity-by-large-margin/.

Bibliography

This bibliography lists a selection of the main sources used in this book. Full details of all sources are provided in the endnotes.

Aas, Katja, *Globalisation and Crime*, 2nd edn (London: Sage, 2019)

Archer, Dane, and Rosemary Gartner, *Violence and Crime in Cross-National Perspective* (New Haven, CT: Yale University Press, 1984)

Bardon, Jonathan, *A History of Ulster* (Belfast: Blackstaff, 1992)

Bayley, David, 'Post-Conflict Police Reform: Is Northern Ireland a model?', *Policing*, vol. 2, no. 2, 2008, pp. 233–40

Bew, Paul, Peter Gibbon and Henry Patterson, *Northern Ireland 1921–2001: Political power and social classes*, 3rd edn (London: Serif, 2002)

Boal, Frederick, and Neville Douglas (eds), *Integration and Division: Geographical perspectives on the Northern Ireland problem* (London: Academic Press, 1982)

Boyle, Kevin, Tom Hadden and Paddy Hillyard, *Law and State: The case of Northern Ireland* (London: Martin Robertson, 1975)

———, *Ten Years On: The legal control of political violence* (London: Cobden Trust, 1980)

Brewer, John D., Bill Lockhart and Paula Rodgers, *Crime in Ireland 1945–1995: Here be Dragons* (Oxford: Clarendon, 1997)

———, 'Informal Social Control and Crime Management in Belfast', *British Journal of Sociology*, vol. 49, no. 4, 1998, pp. 570–85

Brewer, John D., with Kathleen Magee, *Inside the RUC: Routine policing in a divided society* (Oxford: Clarendon, 1991)

Bruce, Steve, *The Red Hand: Protestant paramilitaries in Northern Ireland* (Oxford: Oxford University Press, 1992)

Byrne, Jonny, and John Topping, *Community Safety: A decade of development, delivery, challenge and change in Northern Ireland* (Belfast: Belfast Conflict Resolution Consortium, 2012)

Byrne, Jonny, and Lisa Monaghan, *Policing Republican and Loyalist Communities: Understanding key issues for local communities and the PSNI* (Belfast: Institute for Conflict Research, 2008)

Cadwallader, Anne, *Lethal Allies: British collusion in Ireland* (Dublin: Mercier Press, 2013)

Cairns, Ed, *Caught in the Crossfire: Children and the Northern Ireland conflict* (Belfast: Appletree Press, 1987)

Cameron Report, *Disturbances in Northern Ireland: Report of the commission appointed by the governor of Northern Ireland*, Cmd 532 (Belfast: Stationery Office, 1969)

Campbell, P., A. Rice and K. Ross, *Experience of Crime: Findings from the 2019/20 Northern Ireland Safe Community Survey* (Belfast: Department of Justice, 2021)

Carrington, Kerry, Russell Hogg, John Scott and Maximo Sozzo (eds), *The Palgrave Handbook of Criminology and the Global South* (London: Palgrave Macmillan, 2018)

Caul, Brian, John Pinkerton and Fred Powell (eds), *The Juvenile Justice System in Northern Ireland* (Newtownabbey: Ulster Polytechnic, 1983)

Consultative Group on the Past, *Report of the Consultative Group on the Past* (Belfast: Stationery Office, 2009)

Corcoran, Mary, *Out of Order: The political imprisonment of women in Northern Ireland 1972–1998* (Cullompton: Willan, 2006)

Criminal Justice Review Group, *Review of the Criminal Justice System in Northern Ireland* (Belfast: Stationery Office, 2000)

Darby, John, *Intimidation and the Control of Conflict in Northern Ireland* (Dublin: Gill & Macmillan, 1986)

David, Lea, *The Past Can't Heal Us: The dangers of mandating memory in the name of human rights* (Cambridge: Cambridge University Press, 2020)

Donohue, Laura, 'Regulating Northern Ireland: The Special Powers Acts, 1922–1972', *The Historical Journal*, vol. 41, no. 4, 1998, pp. 1089–120

Dudai, Ron, 'Informers and the Transition in Northern Ireland', *British Journal of Criminology*, vol. 52, no. 1, 2012, pp. 32–54

Ellison, Graham, 'A Blueprint for Democratic Policing Anywhere in the World? Police reform, political transition, and conflict resolution in Northern Ireland', *Police Quarterly*, vol. 10, no. 3, 2007, pp. 243–69

————, and Jim Smyth, *The Crowned Harp: Policing Northern Ireland* (London: Pluto, 2000)

English, Richard, *Armed Struggle: The history of the IRA* (London: Pan, 2005)

Eriksson, Anna, *Justice in Transition: Community restorative justice in Northern Ireland* (Cullompton: Willan, 2009)

Farrell, Michael, *Northern Ireland: The Orange state*, 2nd edn (London: Pluto, 1980)

————, *Arming the Protestants: The formation of the Ulster Special Constabulary and the Royal Ulster Constabulary 1920–27* (Dingle: Brandon Books, 1983)

Flackes, W.D., and Sydney Elliott, *Northern Ireland: A political directory, 1968–1993*, 4th edn (Belfast: Blackstaff, 2004)

Greer, Steven, *Supergrasses: A study in anti-terrorist law enforcement in Northern Ireland* (Oxford: Oxford University Press, 1995)

————, and Anthony White, *Abolishing the Diplock Courts* (London: Cobden Trust, 1986)

Gregory, Ian, Niall Cunningham, C. Lloyd, Ian Shuttleworth and Paul Ell, *Troubled Geographies: A spatial history of religion and society in Ireland* (Bloomington, IN: Indiana University Press, 2013)

Hamill, Heather, *The Hoods: Crime and punishment in Belfast* (Princeton, NJ: Princeton University Press, 2011)

Harris, Rosemary, *Prejudice and Tolerance in Ulster: A study of neighbours and 'strangers' in a border community*, 2nd edn (Manchester: Manchester University Press, 1986)

Hayes, Bernadette, and Ian McAllister, 'Sowing Dragon's Teeth: Public support for political violence and paramilitarism in Northern Ireland', *Political Studies*, vol. 49, no. 5, 2001, pp. 901–22

Helsinki Watch, *Children in Northern Ireland: Abused by security forces and paramilitaries* (New York: Human Rights Watch, 1992)

Heskin, Ken, 'Societal Disintegration in Northern Ireland: Fact or fiction?', *Economic and Social Review*, vol. 12, no. 2, 1981, pp. 93–113

Hillyard, Paddy, 'The Normalization of Special Powers: From Northern Ireland to Britain', in Phil Scraton (ed.), *Law, Order and the Authoritarian State* (Milton Keynes: Open University Press, 1987)

Historical Institutional Abuse Inquiry, *Report of the Historical Institutional Abuse Inquiry* (10 volumes) (Belfast: Stationery Office, 2017), www.hiainquiry.org.

Hourigan, Niamh, John F. Morrison, James Windle and Andrew Silke, 'Crime in Ireland North and South: Feuding gangs and profiteering paramilitaries', *Trends in Organised Crime*, vol. 21, no. 2, 2018, pp. 126–46

Independent Commission on Policing (ICP), *A New Beginning: Policing in Northern Ireland – Report of the Independent Commission on Policing for Northern Ireland* (Belfast: Stationery Office, 1999)

Jackson, John, and Sean Doran, *Judge Without Jury: Diplock trials in the adversary system* (Oxford: Clarendon, 1995)

Jamieson, Ruth (ed.), *The Criminology of War* (Abingdon: Routledge, 2016)

Jarman, Neil, 'From War to Peace? Changing patterns of violence in Northern Ireland, 1990–2003', *Terrorism and Political Violence*, vol. 16, no. 3, 2004, pp. 420–38

Kitson, Frank, *Low-Intensity Operations: Subversion, insurgency and peacekeeping*, 2nd edn (London: Faber & Faber, 1989)

Knox, Colin, '"See No Evil, Hear No Evil": Insidious paramilitary violence in Northern Ireland', *British Journal of Criminology*, vol. 42, no. 1, 2002, pp. 164–85

Lawther, Cheryl, *Truth, Denial and Transition: Northern Ireland and the contested past* (Abingdon: Routledge, 2014)

Leahy, Thomas, *The Intelligence War Against the IRA* (Cambridge: Cambridge University Press, 2020)

Lundy, Patricia, 'Paradoxes and Challenges of Transitional Justice at the "Local" Level: Historical enquiries in Northern Ireland', *Contemporary Social Science*, vol. 6, no. 1, 2011, pp. 89–105

Malešević, Siniša, *The Sociology of War and Violence* (Cambridge: Cambridge University Press, 2010)

Mayhew, Pat, and Jan van Dijk, *Crime Victimisation in Eleven Industrialised Countries: Key findings from the 1996 International Crime Victims Survey* (The Hague: WODC, 1997)

McAlinden, Anne-Marie, and Clare Dwyer (eds), *Criminal Justice in Transition: The Northern Ireland context* (Oxford: Hart, 2015)

McCullough, Dave, Tanja Schmidt and Bill Lockhart, *Car Theft in Northern Ireland: Recent studies on a persistent problem* (Belfast: Extern Organisation, 1990)

McEvoy, Kieran, *Paramilitary Imprisonment in Northern Ireland: Resistance, management and release* (Oxford: Clarendon, 2001)

McGarry, John, and Brendan O'Leary, *Explaining Northern Ireland* (Oxford: Blackwell, 1995)

McGovern, Mark, *Counterinsurgency and Collusion in Northern Ireland* (London: Pluto, 2019)

McKittrick, David, Seamus Kelters, Brian Feeney, Chris Thornton and David McVea, *Lost Lives: The stories of the men and women who died as a result of the Northern Ireland Troubles*, revised edn (London: Mainstream, 2007)

Mitchell, Claire, *Religion, Identity and Belonging in Northern Ireland: Boundaries of belonging and belief* (Farnham: Ashgate, 2006)

Moloney, Ed, *A Secret History of the IRA* (London: Penguin, 2003)

Monaghan, Rachel, '"An Imperfect Peace": Paramilitary "punishments" in Northern Ireland', *Terrorism and Political Violence*, vol. 16, no. 3, 2004, pp. 439–61

Moore, Linda, and Phil Scraton, *The Incarceration of Women: Punishing bodies, breaking spirits* (Basingstoke: Palgrave Macmillan, 2014)

Moran, Jon, *Policing the Peace in Northern Ireland: Politics, crime and security after the Belfast Agreement* (Manchester: Manchester University Press, 2008)

Mulcahy, Aogán, *Policing Northern Ireland: Conflict, legitimacy and reform* (Cullompton: Willan/Routledge, 2006)

——, 'Great Expectations and Complex Realities: Assessing the impact and implications of police reform in Northern Ireland', in

Jennifer Brown (ed.), *The Future of Policing* (Abingdon: Routledge, 2013)

Munck, Ronnie, 'The Lads and the Hoods: Alternative justice in an Irish context', in Mike Tomlinson, Tony Varley and Ciaran McCullagh (eds), *Whose Law and Order?* (Belfast: Sociological Association of Ireland, 1988)

Nelken, David, *Comparative Criminal Justice* (London: Sage, 2010)

Ó Dochartaigh, Niall, *Deniable Contact: Back-channel negotiation in Northern Ireland* (Oxford: Oxford University Press, 2021)

O'Dowd, Liam, Bill Roiston and Mike Tomlinson, *Northern Ireland: Between civil rights and civil war* (London: CSE Books, 1980)

O'Leary, Brendan, and John McGarry, *The Politics of Antagonism: Understanding Northern Ireland*, 2nd edn (London: Athlone Press, 1996)

O'Mahony, David, Ray Geary, Kieran McEvoy and John Morison, *Crime, Community and Locale: The Northern Ireland Communities Crime Survey* (Aldershot: Ashgate, 2000)

Oversight Commissioner, *Overseeing the Proposed Revisions for the Policing Services of Northern Ireland – Report 19 (Final Report)* (Belfast: Office of the Oversight Commissioner, 2007)

Parkinson, Alan, *Belfast's Unholy Wars: The Troubles of the 1920s* (Dublin: Four Courts Press, 2004)

Punch, Maurice, *State Violence, Collusion and the Troubles: Counterinsurgency, government deviance and Northern Ireland* (London: Pluto, 2012)

Purdie, Bob, *Politics in the Streets: The origins of the civil rights movement in Northern Ireland* (Belfast: Blackstaff Press, 1990)

Rolston, Bill, and Mairead Gilmartin, *Unfinished Business: State killings and the quest for truth* (Belfast: Beyond the Pale, 2000)

Rose, Richard, *Governing Without Consensus* (London: Faber & Faber, 1971)

Ryder, Chris, *The RUC, 1922–2000* (London: Arrow, 2000)

Scarman Tribunal, *Violence and Civil Disturbances in Northern Ireland in 1969: Report of tribunal of inquiry*, Cmd 566 (Belfast: Stationery Office, 1972)

Silke, Andrew, and Max Taylor, 'War without End: Comparing IRA and loyalist vigilantism in Northern Ireland', *Howard Journal of Criminal Justice*, vol. 39, no. 3, 2000, pp. 249–66

Smith, David, and Gerry Chambers, *Inequality in Northern Ireland* (Oxford: Clarendon Press, 1991)

Spotlight on the Troubles: A secret history, seven-part BBC television series (2019), available at: youtube.com

Stalker, John, *Stalker* (London: Harrap, 1998)

Stevens, John, *Stevens Enquiry 3: Overview and Recommendations* (London: Stationery Office, 2003), available at: https://cain.ulster. ac.uk/issues/collusion/chron.htm.

Sutton, Malcolm, *An Index of Deaths from the Conflict in Ireland*, University of Ulster, Conflict Archive on the Internet, 2001, available at: http://www.cain.ulst.ac.uk/sutton.

Taylor, Peter, *Beating the Terrorists? Interrogation at Armagh, Gough and Castlereagh* (London: Penguin, 1980)

——, *Provos: The IRA and Sinn Féin* (London: Bloomsbury, 1998)

——, *Loyalists* (London: Bloomsbury, 2000)

——, *Brits: The war against the IRA* (London: Bloomsbury, 2001)

Todd, Jennifer, *Identity Change After Conflict: Ethnicity, boundaries and belonging in the two Irelands* (London: Palgrave Macmillan, 2018)

Tomlinson, Mike, 'Policing the New Europe: The Northern Ireland factor', in Tony Bunyan (ed.), *Statewatching the New Europe* (London: Statewatch, 1993), pp. 87–114

van Dijk, Jan, and Patricia Mayhew, *Criminal Victimisation in the Industrialised World: Key findings of the 1989 and 1992 International Crime Surveys* (The Hague: Ministry of Justice, 1993)

van Dijk, Jan, John van Kesteren and Paul Smit, *Criminal Victimisation in International Perspective: Key findings from the 2004–2005 ICVS and EU ICS* (The Hague: Ministry of Justice, 2007)

van Kesteren, John, Pat Mayhew and Paul Nieuwbeerta, *Criminal Victimisation in Seventeen Industrialised Countries: Key findings from the 2000 International Crime Victims Survey* (The Hague: Ministry of Justice, 2000)

Walklate, Sandra, and Ross McGarry (eds), *Criminology and War: Transgressing the Borders* (Abingdon: Routledge, 2015)

Walsh, Dermot, *The Use and Abuse of Emergency Legislation in Northern Ireland* (London: Cobden Trust, 1983)

Weitzer, Ronald, *Policing Under Fire: Ethnic conflict and police–community relations in Northern Ireland* (Albany: State University of New York Press, 1995)

Whyte, John, 'How Much Discrimination Was There Under the Unionist Regime, 1921–1968?', in Tom Gallagher and James O'Connell (eds), *Contemporary Irish Studies* (Manchester: Manchester University Press, 1983), pp. 1–36

———, *Interpreting Northern Ireland* (Oxford: Clarendon, 1990)

Wilson, Tim, *Frontiers of Violence: Conflict and identity in Ulster and Upper Silesia 1918–1922* (Oxford: Oxford University Press, 2010)

———, '"The Most Terrible Assassination That Has Yet Stained the Name of Belfast": The McMahon murders in context', *Irish Historical Studies*, vol. 37, no. 145, 2010, pp. 83–106

Index

Note: Page locators in bold refer to figures and tables.